The church of the future must b
model of a church like Antioch. In Jeff
you can learn what it means to be a tra
not only sound theologically, but aggre
and making disciples of all the nations. Read it and grow personally. Share it and change another leader and his church.

Dr. Ronnie W. Floyd, Senior Pastor
Cross Church, Northwest Arkansas

In a day when the church in North America is more of an event
we attend than a community of life-change to which we belong,
Jeff Iorg has provided a great measuring stick for New Testament
community. I thank God for his challenge to the church and pray it
will move the Body of Christ to be on mission to change the world!

Vance Pitman, Senior Pastor
Hope Baptist Church, Las Vegas, Nevada

How to revitalize an underperforming church is the number
problem facing pastors today. Jeff Iorg offers a biblical, practical
strategy born out of his own experience of building a transforming
church in a secular, unchurched setting.

Don't read the table of contents unless you are ready to read
the book. You will find it addresses the challenges your church is
facing this week. This one really is useful. I have no higher praise.

Chuck Kelley, President
New Orleans Baptist Theological Seminary

Reading a book by Dr. Jeff Iorg is like going to a counselor and
inspirational conference all at once. He has the ability to encourage
and challenge in the same paragraph. If you are a leader wanting
to sharper your heart and skill, you have come to the right place."

Gregg Matte, Pastor
Houston's First Baptist Church, Houston, Texas

"A picture is worth a thousand words." If this celebrated quote is true, Jeff Iorg has provided the twenty-first century church with a picture of inestimable value. In The Case for Antioch, the postmodern church is about to behold a replicable model of a healthy church. While no church is perfect, your church can prove and improve its health by intentionally becoming a transformational church. Jeff Iorg engagingly points the church in the right direction through this relevant biblical case study.

Claybon Lea Jr., D.Min., President,
California State Baptist Convention, Inc.

Reading this book, one will see beautiful antiques on display in a contemporary store. In this brilliant work, Dr. Iorg takes us "back to the future" helping the reader anticipate a bright future for the evangelical church; if we are ready to "do church" with the Antioch model in mind. Today's evangelical church is fighting battles on all fronts, and seems to be losing these battles. The author takes us back to the beginning, when the church was able to stand up to the world. Here is an account of what the Christians of the first century believed, and practiced, and how their model can be implemented in today's church. This is not primarily a historical book, but rather a fresh, creative look at the needs of the contemporary church. It is a call to all church leaders and members to return to the simple holiness, unfailing love, and patient cross-bearing of the early Christians. The Case for Antioch, written with sound scholarship and free-flowing style, is an excellent tool for contemporary evangelicals. This book will help you find traditional biblical answers to modern day problems in all areas of church life. You will be challenged to a deeper walk with Jesus—the walk of the early Christians.

—John Brisc, Pastor
Romanian Baptist Church, Portland, Oregon

THE CASE FOR
ANTIOCH

THE CASE FOR

ANTIOCH

A Biblical Model for a **TRANSFORMATIONAL CHURCH**

JEFF IORG

PUBLISHING GROUP

NASHVILLE, TENNESSEE

978-1-4336-7138-8

Published by B&H Publishing Group,
Nashville, Tennessee

Dewey Decimal Classification: 250
Subject Heading: CHURCH RENEWAL \
CHURCH—BIBLICAL TEACHING \ ANTIOCH
(TURKEY)—CHURCH HISTORY

4 5 6 7 8 9 10 • 17 16 15 14 13

Dedication

To the founding families of
Greater Gresham Baptist Church
in Gresham, Oregon,
who pursued our shared vision
with passion and sacrifice;
and to
Joe Flegal and Keith Evans,
two pastoral leaders who
turned the dream into
a community-changing reality.

Contents

Foreword

It matters that the church be transformational. Both among the people who comprise its membership and in its effect toward the surrounding community, the local church is a tool for life transformation to the glory of God.

In this second volume of the Transformational Church series, Jeff Iorg uses the church at Antioch as a case model for what many consider the model missional church in the New Testament. As the third largest city in the Roman Empire, Antioch had much in common with today's cities. Iorg writes, "Antioch was a large, complex, multicultural, city—a perfect precursor to the missional setting of the church in the twenty-first century." Our world is becoming complex and multicultural, but the answer still remains the same.

God has chosen the church to make known His manifold wisdom. In His sovereign plan, God uses the church and its imperfect members for His perfect plan. Yet, even the believers in the New Testament were flawed and frail, like us. Yet, one church has a consistent good reputation in the New Testament—the church at Antioch. The New Testament tells of its troubles and triumphs.

Jeff Iorg has chosen to tell the story of Antioch in the context of the overall struggles, challenges, and triumphs of the larger first-century church context. Struggles with the law, inclusion of the Gentiles into the body of Christ, and missionary outreach were the context surrounding this city where the disciples were first called Christians. Again we see a similar context to our time with our expanding, yet changing missionary outreach, a shift in the global center of God's kingdom, as well as economic upheavals, cultural challenges, and religious pluralism.

Does God's Word have a message for churches in our time? Jeff answers with a resounding, "Yes!" and that word can be found in the example of the church at Antioch. With a ministry background well out of the comfort of the "Bible Belt"—having pastored in the Pacific Northwest and leading a seminary in San Francisco—Jeff Iorg is uniquely qualified to address this subject.

Thom Rainer and I noted in the first book in this series, "The concepts of *transformation* and *church* play off each other, complement each other, connect to each other. And when you put not just the nouns transformation and church together . . . but put together the actual occurrence of transformation and the community of people called church, the result is powerful. . . . [It's] transformation and church the way God designed them to be."[1]

I encourage you to read and apply the concepts presented in these pages so our churches might be more effective than ever at getting the gospel to those in desperate need of its life transforming power.

Ed Stetzer

Part 1

A Biblical Case Study

Chapter 1
_____

A Biblical Model of a Transformational Church

Someday I pray I will pastor
a New Testament church.

—Jeff Iorg, age 19

❖ God answered my prayer! He allowed me to lead two New Testament churches for more than thirteen years. Sometimes it might be best if God spared us by answering some of our youthful prayers with a resounding *no!* But in my case He answered *yes* and allowed me to experience the gamut of pastoral leadership in two contrasting settings—as pastor of a traditional church in a conservative community and church-planting pastor in a secular city.

In my idealistic zeal to pastor a church modeled after those described in the Bible (as I imagined them), it never occurred to me to study the New Testament churches *before* praying to pastor one like them. My naïve assumption was that biblical church life was idyllic—with the early church following Jesus "from victory unto victory" as a historic hymn suggests. During college and seminary courses, I discovered the truth about those memorable congregations. With rare exception they were a mess! Moral failure, doctrinal divisions, personality cults, and divisive fellowship were the norm. That's why, as it turned out, the churches I served *were* New Testament churches. They, no we, were a mess—starting with the pastor and including everyone from the preschoolers to the patriarchs. We were similar to many New Testament churches at one time or another and in one dysfunctional way or another.

This may sound like a diatribe against my former churches. It's not. The church (expressed as local churches) is God's eternal plan, the summation of His redemptive work, and its glorification the culmination of history. Local churches, warts and all, are God's strategy for advancing His kingdom. The incredible and certain future of the church means giving your life in church leadership is a worthwhile investment. Taking an honest look at first-century churches doesn't diminish their significance or the value we place on churches today. Instead, it increases our appreciation for churches, then and now, by giving us a more realistic vision of actual church life. First-century churches were flawed, *but they also changed their world and ours.*

In today's church we seem to have the "flawed" part down pat. It's the "change the world" part we are struggling to emulate. While many biblical churches had struggles and shortcomings, their portrayal paints a backdrop for understanding one remarkable New Testament congregation presented as a healthier model—First Church, Antioch. While it also had its problems, it rose above them to change its world and ours, extending its influence through the centuries. To understand how remarkable this church really was, let's overview the record of some other first-century churches.

New Testament Churches

Consider first, the church at Corinth. It had so many problems it required two lengthy Pauline letters to confront its myriad dysfunctions. It had a member who was having an incestuous relationship with his stepmother (1 Cor. 5). The worship services were a three-ring circus, a free-for-all, with all manner of frivolous and irreverent public displays (1 Cor. 11–12). They weren't only fractious in worship but also factionalized in camps following various leaders (1 Cor. 1, 3). Christians were suing one another (1 Cor. 6) and confused about marriage and related relationships (1 Cor. 7). That part sounds a lot like today! The Corinthians, while generous, had significant financial issues related to giving and receiving offerings (2 Cor. 8–9). Sprinkled throughout the Corinthian letters are additional instructions and corrections about a host of other theological and methodological church problems.

The church in Rome also had its struggles with sin (Rom. 1), although perhaps not as pronounced as in Corinth. The Roman church apparently had profound doctrinal questions, which occasioned some of Paul's most thorough theological writing comprising the bulk of his letter to them. The Romans also struggled with practical problems like church/state relationships (Rom. 13) and church fellowship/function issues (Rom. 12). Paul concluded his letter by connecting theology with practice, addressing common church problems and solutions based on sound doctrine (Rom. 14–15).

The churches in Galatia battled over the nature of the gospel (Gal. 1–2), the role of the law (Gal. 3), and freedom of conscience (Gal. 5). The Ephesians struggled with the nature of the church—universal church or local church. As part of this, they were also confused about the function of church leaders (Eph. 4), the application of the gospel in domestic relationships (Eph. 5–6), and the nature of spiritual warfare (Eph. 6). The Philippians had fellowship issues, memorialized by two women, Euodia and Syntyche, in such conflict they were singled out by name! (Phil. 4:2). What could have caused such a divisive conflict that Paul addressed it, under inspiration, in an open letter to be read to the church (and later included in the Canon)? That must have been some fight!

The church at Thessalonica was confused about the second coming of the Lord, some members having retreated to a mountaintop to await his return (1 Thess. 5; 2 Thess. 2). The Colossians struggled to understand the deity of Jesus (Col. 1–2). Both Timothy and Titus, local church pastors, received extensive instructions in letters addressed to them (and their churches). These correctives weren't random Pauline musings but were written against the backdrop of actual church leadership challenges those men faced.

When considering the seven churches of the Revelation, things aren't much different. While some of the churches escaped criticism, most were called out for specific shortcomings. The Ephesians had, about thirty years after receiving Paul's letter extolling the church (Eph. 3), abandoned their love for Jesus (Rev. 2:4). In Pergamum, the church had succumbed to false teachers, the Nicolaitans, and was sternly warned to repent before any hope for doctrinal recovery was forfeited (Rev. 3:16). The church at Thyatira tolerated a "Jezebel" who was disrupting their fellowship by eating meat sacrificed to idols and practicing sexual immorality (Rev. 2:20). While barely alive, the Sardis church was spiritually deceived—thinking they were thriving, though nearly dead—and warned to wake up quickly (Rev. 3:2). And finally, infamously, the church at Laodicea was lukewarm—nauseatingly tepid—and in danger of being vomited out of the Lord's mouth (Rev. 2:16).

These are a sampling of New Testament churches. Which one would you like to lead? When I prayed to pastor a New Testament church, I had no idea what I was asking. Those churches were a diverse collection of dysfunctional believers trying to work out the messy first decades of community life in Christ. Most of what was written to those churches reveals their problems, struggles, and inadequacies. The New Testament chronicles church fights, doctrinal rifts, worship tensions, and interpersonal conflicts in almost all named churches. By and large, the early churches had a plethora of troubling, disheartening, passion-killing problems that make potential leaders (or members) shudder.

But there was one exception, one beautiful exception. One transformational church overcame formidable obstacles to model healthy, balanced, effective church life. *This* is the New Testament church we all dream of creating, joining, or leading.

First Church, Antioch

The story of the church at Antioch is an inspiring drama, a model of a transformational church in the first century for the church in the twenty-first century. Antioch is an ancient model for the future church. This church, composed of transformed people, transformed its community, the Mediterranean region, and the world as we know it. We are fortunate to have an extensive biblical record of its beginning and early years of growth, along with examples of how it handled doctrinal debates, personality conflicts, and practical matters of church life, Christian devotion, and missionary outreach. This record provides a case study for starting and growing transformational churches. Here then, with some bridging comments, is the story of the church at Antioch as recorded in the New Testament.

When the early Christian movement was about ten to fifteen years old,[2] still largely focused on Jewish evangelism and centered in the church at Jerusalem, trouble erupted and . . .

> Those who had been scattered as a result of the persecution that started because of Stephen made their way as far as Phoenicia, Cyprus, and Antioch, speaking the message to no one except Jews. But there were some of them, Cypriot and Cyrenian men, who came to Antioch and began speaking to the Hellenists, proclaiming the good news about the Lord Jesus. The Lord's hand was with them, and a large number who believed turned to the Lord. Then the report about them reached the ears of the church in Jerusalem, and they sent out Barnabas to travel as far as Antioch. When he arrived and saw the grace of God, he was glad, and he encouraged all of them to remain true to the Lord with a firm resolve of the heart—for he was a good man, full of the Holy Spirit and of faith—and large numbers of people were added to the Lord. Then he went to Tarsus to search for Saul, and when he found him he brought him to Antioch. For a whole year they met with the church and taught large numbers, and the disciples were first called Christians in Antioch. In those days some prophets came down from Jerusalem to Antioch. . . .
>
> Then one of them, named Agabus, stood up and predicted by the Spirit that there would be a severe famine throughout the Roman world. This took place during the time of Claudius. So each of the disciples, according to his ability, determined to send relief to the brothers who lived in Judea. This they did, sending it to the elders by means of Barnabas and Saul. (Acts 11:19–30)

Barnabas and Saul took the offering to Jerusalem and distributed it. After some time had passed, they returned to Antioch and resumed their leadership roles.

> In the local church at Antioch there were prophets and teachers: Barnabas, Simeon who was called Niger, Lucius the Cyrenian, Manaen, a close friend of Herod the tetrarch, and Saul. As they were ministering to the Lord and fasting, the Holy Spirit said,

"Set apart for Me Barnabas and Saul for the work that I have
called them to." Then, after they had fasted, prayed, and laid
hands on them, they sent them off. (Acts 13:1–3)

The first missionary team intentionally sent by a local church
to extend the gospel throughout the Gentile world moved out on
their first trip. After profitable work in several cities, they stopped
in Attalia.

From there they sailed back to Antioch where they had been
entrusted to the grace of God for the work they had completed.
After they arrived and gathered the church together, they
reported everything God had done with them, and that He had
opened the door of faith to the Gentiles. And they spent a considerable time with the disciples. (Acts 14:26–28)

While the team traveled, trouble was brewing in the Jerusalem
church. Some brothers were upset about the news that Gentiles
were becoming Christians without first becoming Jews. The
problem came to a head in Antioch.

Some men came down from Judea and began to teach the
brothers: "Unless you are circumcised according to the custom
prescribed by Moses, you cannot be saved!" But after Paul and
Barnabas had engaged them in serious argument and debate,
they arranged for Paul and Barnabas and some others of them
to go up to the apostles and elders in Jerusalem concerning
this controversy. When they had been sent on their way by
the church, they passed through both Phoenicia and Samaria,
explaining in detail the conversion of the Gentiles, and they created great joy among all the brothers. (Acts 15:1–3)

The phrase "serious argument and debate" doesn't do justice to
the conflict. Paul described the conflict this way:

This issue arose because of false brothers smuggled in, who
came in secretly to spy on our freedom that we have in Christ

Jesus, in order to enslave us. But we did not yield in submission to these people for even an hour, so that the truth of the gospel would remain for you. (Gal. 2:4–5)

The Jerusalem Council hashed out the problem and decided salvation by grace through faith alone was the true gospel. They selected a team of respected leaders to deliver their conclusion to Antioch, along with a letter calling for deference in matters of conscience effecting Christian fellowship. The letter was sent . . .

From the apostles and the elders, your brothers,
To the brothers from among the Gentiles in Antioch, Syria, and Cilicia: Greetings. Because we have heard that some to whom we gave no authorization went out from us and troubled you with their words and unsettled your hearts, we have unanimously decided to select men and send them to you along with our beloved Barnabas and Paul, who have risked their lives for the name of our Lord Jesus Christ. Therefore we have sent Judas and Silas, who will personally report the same things by word of mouth. For it was the Holy Spirit's decision—and ours—to put no greater burden on you than these necessary things: that you abstain from food offered to idols, from blood, from eating anything that has been strangled, and from sexual immorality. If you keep yourselves from these things, you will do well. Farewell. (Acts 15:23–29)

With the letter in hand, a delegation prepared to deliver the defining document which settled the controversy over the nature of the gospel. With the blessing of the Jerusalem church,

Then, being sent off, they went down to Antioch, and after gathering the assembly, they delivered the letter. When they read it, they rejoiced because of its encouragement. Both Judas and Silas, who were also prophets themselves, encouraged the brothers and strengthened them with a long message. After spending some time there, they were sent back in peace by the brothers to those who had sent them. But Paul and Barnabas, along with many others, remained in Antioch teaching and proclaiming the message of the Lord. (Acts 15:30–35)

Solving this problem was very important to the early church and for the future of the gospel. Working through these issues wasn't easy. Sometimes public antagonism erupted between prominent leaders. The intensity of the issue is illustrated by a conflict between Peter and Paul sometime during this process.[3] Paul told the Galatians about it this way.

But when Cephas came to Antioch, I opposed him to his face because he stood condemned. For he used to eat with the Gentiles before certain men came from James. However, when they came, he withdrew and separated himself, because he feared those from the circumcision party. Then the rest of the Jews joined his hypocrisy, so that even Barnabas was carried away by their hypocrisy. But when I saw that they were deviating from the truth of the gospel, I told Cephas in front of everyone, "If you, who are a Jew, live like a Gentile and not like a Jew, how can you compel Gentiles to live like Jews?" (Gal. 2:11–14)

Once these theological issues were resolved, the missionary team was ready to return to their primary work of spreading the gospel among the Gentiles. But first, a thorny personnel problem had to be resolved.

After some time had passed, Paul said to Barnabas, "Let's go back and visit the brothers in every town where we have preached the message of the Lord, and see how they're doing." Barnabas wanted to take along John Mark. But Paul did not think it appropriate to take along this man who had deserted them in Pamphylia and had not gone on with them to the work. There was such a sharp disagreement that they parted company, and Barnabas took Mark with him and sailed off to Cyprus. Then Paul chose Silas and departed, after being commended to the grace of the Lord by the brothers. He traveled through Syria and Cilicia, strengthening the churches. (Acts 15:36–41)

Two missionary teams resulted from this bitter conflict between former colleagues. Eventually, Paul (along with Silas) came back, stopping at Jerusalem, and then . . .

> On landing at Caesarea, he went up and greeted the church, and went down to Antioch. (Acts 18:22)

It was a brief stopover, a quick report, and then the Antioch church launched Paul on his third missionary journey, his last before his extended trip that landed him in a Roman prison.

> He set out, traveling through one place after another in the Galatian territory and Phrygia, strengthening all the disciples. (Acts 18:23)

What a remarkable story! We have a detailed account of this amazing congregation—the first predominantly Gentile church—from its birth through its role in launching the gospel toward Rome (then the most important city in the Mediterranean world). Before we look in detail at this story and analyze the qualities which made this such a remarkable church, let's consider its setting. This is vital because the context for the church at Antioch is a significant reason it is a model church for today.

Where was this ancient city, the fertile ground from which this remarkable church emerged? What was the city like? Why was Antioch the perfect place (particularly considering our world today) for the first Gentile church to flourish? What makes this church's story so applicable to the twenty-first century? What about Antioch's setting predicates the possibility of developing a transformational church in our secular, irreligious world?

Ancient Antioch

Antioch was a large, complex, pluralistic, multicultural city—a perfect precursor to the missional setting of the church in the twenty-first century. The world's population is moving to the cities, and future kingdom growth must be fueled by city-based churches and church-planting movements. In 2008, the worldwide population in urban areas exceeded the population in rural areas for the first time in human history. By 2030, more than five billion people will live in the world's cities, far eclipsing the remaining rural population. The number of large cities and the size of megacities are both increasing rapidly. By 2015, there will be more than five hundred cities with a population of more than one million people each. And, by that same year, there will be twenty-two megacities with more than ten million people living in them.[4] Population trends mandate the future church be effective in the world's cities.

The church, in almost every global setting, has been stronger in rural areas, small towns, and suburbs than in major cities and metropolitan areas. There are several reasons for this. Modern cities are sometimes perceived as outposts of concentrated evil to be avoided by Christians. Churches have often vacated inner-city property rather than deal with changing ethnic population patterns. Church flight has also occurred as cities have changed and become inhospitable to traditional church forms and functions. Starting new churches or maintaining healthy churches in urban environments is difficult, usually more so than in other settings because of the additional challenges of city life. For example, financing new church starts, even the most basic expense of providing housing for a church planter, is expensive in cities.

As the world becomes more urbanized, developing city-focused strategies for effective church planting and ministry is essential. That's why Antioch is such an important setting for understanding church life today. Antioch was a city church—a paradigm-shifting, world-changing, missionally effective movement of God in a major population center. The church at Antioch inspires us because it was birthed and functioned effectively in an urban environment. If the future church is effective, it must thrive in the mission field of the twenty-first-century cities. If the gospel is successfully planted in major cities, it will spread throughout a country or region (following the overall pattern of the book of Acts).

What was Antioch like? It was the third largest city in the Roman Empire with a population estimated between 500,000 and 800,000. Imagine a city that size before indoor plumbing, comprehensive sewage systems, and systematized garbage collection and disposal! Despite what it lacked in modern conveniences, it was a beautiful city laid out in a grid pattern with streets positioned to take advantage of cool afternoon breezes. It was located near the mouth of the Orontes River, about fifteen miles from its port city of Seleucus, making Antioch both an inland city and a major seaport.[5] The location is now Antakya, Turkey, about twelve miles from the Syrian border.

Antioch was a Roman city with a prominent Greek heritage. Founded in 300 BC as the capital of the Seleucid Empire, it came under Roman jurisdiction in 64 BC. It was given status as a "free city" by the Roman general Pompey, granting it limited self-government and some exemption from provincial taxes. When the Roman province of Syria was organized in 23 BC, Antioch became the capital, continuing its role as a governmental center.[6]

Antioch was infamous for its religious practices. Five miles from the city was a smaller community, Daphne. It was a cult center for the worship of Artemis, Apollos, and Astarte. Worship practices included temple prostitution, thus the area was known throughout the Roman Empire for its moral laxity.[7] Juvenal wrote, "The sewage of the Syrian Orontes has for long been discharged into the Tiber" (*Satire* 3.62).[8] Antioch was also a center for the worship of Zeus, Poseidon, Adonis, and Tyche[9]—a cosmopolitan city of religious pluralism worshipping a pantheon of gods and goddesses. Part of the religious diversity included a small Jewish community between twenty-five thousand and fifty thousand people, the monotheistic exception to the prevailing amalgam of polytheistic religious practices.[10]

Antioch was also a multicultural stewpot. Greeks, Syrians, Phoenicians, Jews, Arabs, Persians, and Italians were all part of the city's population mix.[11] As a port city, a capital city, and a transportation hub, Antioch attracted all kinds of people creating a cosmopolitan mosaic of nationalities, languages, and cultures.

In summary, Antioch was a large city with many of the characteristics of today's cities and megacities. Antioch had a pluralistic population both ethnically and religiously. It was located on a river, near a seaport, thus fueling its diversity and ever-changing character. Many of the problems of large cities—from moral depravity to economic disparity to racial tension—were no doubt evident. The city carried a proud identity as a free city and was self-determining, in some ways having an identity exceeding any national or regional connection. In that regard Antioch was a lot like San Francisco, Rio de Janeiro, Paris, or Cairo.

But unlike most modern cities, the gospel thrived in Antioch. As our world becomes more urbanized, we must have confidence the gospel can change lives and transformational churches can grow in cities. Where people live in the greatest density, the problems of humanity intensify. Sin abounds in cities. Yet, where sin abounds, grace abounds all the more. Where grace abounds, the gospel transforms. As the gospel transforms individuals, congregations form to celebrate and spread the gospel. First, Antioch is an inspiring church that changed a city and motivates us to do the same. No place is too large, too diverse, too religiously confused, or too sinful for the gospel. Churches can thrive in cities. Churches can transform cities.

A Case-Study Approach

Before we launch our study of the church at Antioch, let's establish the parameters for developing a transformational church model based on this ancient congregation. Antioch is an example, a model that can be used as a case study. We are fortunate to have a thorough record of this church in the Bible, but we don't have every detail about its form or function. We do have an inspired description, complete with details about crucial incidents and practices, revealing timeless principles about church life. While the biblical narrative about Antioch isn't exhaustive, it is illustrative of many pertinent issues churches have faced over the centuries, continue to encounter, and will grapple with in the future. A case study reveals some insights but not everything about the subject of a case. This is also true of Antioch. It reveals some qualities of a transformational church, but it's not an exhaustive list.

The importance of studying, in some depth, a biblical model shouldn't need to be defended among Christians. But sometimes I wonder! We are enamored with anthropological, cultural, ethnographic, and sociological studies analyzing the church from every perspective possible. We incisively study contemporary examples to discover models to emulate. Dozens of churches package their brand and sell their methods and practices as the sure recipe for church health. Many of these are helpful.

But shouldn't "people of the Book" be more conversant with biblical models, with the principles and patterns of early church life? More than studying these as a theoretical or theological hobby, shouldn't the biblical models profoundly influence the way we "do church"? Shouldn't comparing a church to a biblical model be just as important as knowing how it stacks up against the mean or median statistical standard for churches in its community or denomination? Isn't it more important to imitate a biblical example than mimic the church down the street?

Considering a biblical case study approach to evaluating your church may seem intimidating. You may be predisposed to conclude the biblical standard is perfection and your church won't measure up well. You may be tempted to stop reading because you just don't want to be discouraged any more than you already are.

This book won't beat up your church for its inadequacies (or you for yours). All churches are inadequate, troubled, and less than ideal. So are their leaders. That's not news! From the earliest churches to yours, all churches have been flawed because their members (and leaders) are redeemed, though not yet perfected. Transformational churches rise above those shortcomings, often even capitalizing on them to accomplish amazing results. When you finish this book, you will be energized anew for the continuing challenge of creating a more effective church. As a church leader, or member, any lesser goal will be a waste of your time.

Getting Started

The next chapter outlines a methodology for measuring church health from two broad perspectives. Both are valid. The first, a quantitative approach, is the predominate method used by most analysts today. It makes significant use of statistical data and group comparisons. The second, a more subjective or qualitative approach, is the method we will use in this book. Antioch provides the case study. We can discern principles and patterns that crystallize into qualities of a transformational church by studying this first-century example. This book will help you create a process to measure your church's health—not only by the data but also by *discernible*, observable spiritual realities.

Let's get started.

Chapter 2

Balancing Methods for Measuring Church Health

Determining the relative health of a church is a complicated process. Some try to reduce it to a pass-fail test, creating a grading scale based on statistical variables leading to a definitive conclusion—healthy or unhealthy. It just isn't that simple. While organizations can possibly be measured that way, organisms are more complex. A church is first an organism that expresses itself as an organization. For that reason, diagnosing church health is more art than science. While data matters, so does other information of equal significance.

Diagnosing church health is like practicing medicine. A physician considers multiple variables, some empirical (like test results) and others subjective (based on training, experience, and observation) in determining a patient's relative health. A key phrase is "relative health." Every person has an ever-changing state of health, feeling good one day and not-so-well the next. Health status fluctuates because of many interrelated variables. Churches are living organisms with the same fluidity. Measuring church health requires asking the right diagnostic questions, considering the full range of available information, and accepting a mixed bag of related and sometimes complicated conclusions.

So, how do you decide if your church is healthy? Is it a simple process of looking at the numbers and comparing them to some universal standard? Or is it more a feeling you have based on your perception of spiritual realities? Is it determined by comparing your church's strengths with the other churches in its neighborhood, community, city, or denomination? Or is it more important to compare your church to its potential in its context? If you use an integrated process with multiple variables, how do you combine and evaluate the data objectively and fairly? Just how is church health determined and measured?

Approaches to Answering These Questions

These questions engender debate and sometimes even conflict among church leaders. Some prefer viewing the church solely through an objective lens, collecting and analyzing statistics to reveal a church's strengths and weaknesses. This approach, it is assumed, will lead to black-and-white conclusions resulting in a clear-cut prescription to fix the problems. Others prefer a more subjective approach, relying on anecdotal evidence of spiritual activity, personal growth, and interpersonal development. This method allows for more nuanced analysis and conclusions, acknowledging the complexity of the problems but still working toward concrete solutions.

Which is the better approach? *Neither is better.* Both have merit. Both contribute to a holistic understanding of a church's condition. Both can also be abused by leaders and used to abuse churches. Setting them at odds isn't necessary. Both have value and, when used in combination, can contribute to a thorough analysis and more helpful conclusions. Finding a way to use all available information, objective and subjective, is essential for accurately measuring church health. Like a doctor with a patient, a church-health analyst must use all available information to make an accurate diagnosis.

Some Christians (and even some leaders) reject both options. They resist thinking critically about their ministry setting (and the results they are achieving) because they confuse thinking critically with being a critic. While these words sound similar, their meanings are distinctly different. To think critically means to evaluate thoroughly, objectively, and carefully. To be a critic presumes negativity. Critically considering the condition of your church doesn't presume a negative evaluation. Being honest about your situation, demonstrating integrity in interpreting information, and using all available evaluative tools for constructive improvement rather than destructive critique are part of effective leadership. Measuring church vitality, much like a physician diagnosing a patient, is a means to an end: improved health. This process isn't an autopsy, nor are we hoping to discover terminal conditions. Pastoral leaders practice the cure of souls, not forensic medicine. We are searching for signs of life in our local expression of the body of Christ and want to prescribe treatment to facilitate improved health.

Other leaders continually measure church conditions (almost obsessively), but seem locked into predetermined negative conclusions. They assume, since their church consists of redeemed but not-yet-perfected people, something must be wrong with it. Like the father who is never satisfied with a child's performance, these pastors are never quite satisfied with their church. They communicate—sometimes subtly, other times more overtly—their disdain for their followers' inadequacy. No wonder their efforts to measure church health are resisted. Who wants to be evaluated just to be beaten up? Good leaders take a more balanced, fair approach.

Several years ago a good friend asked me, "Pastor, is something bothering you?"

"No," I replied testily, "why would you ask?"

He said, "Because for the past few weeks, every sermon has felt like an attack—like you are mad at us for some reason."

Ouch! That hurt then and it's painful to write. But my friend was right. My anger at the church for their poor performance on growth-related projects was poisoning my preaching. He gave me some good advice: take a few days off and regain perspective. It was good counsel, and everyone was happier the following Sunday. Be careful as a leader when you evaluate your church. Don't personalize their performance and attack them for making you look bad. Improving church health must be driven by better motives than personal aggrandizement. Our motive must be the well-being of the church and the glory of God, not self-fulfillment or obtaining personal accolades.

Among those who measure church vitality for more positive reasons, denominations and other groups who track church progress tend to focus on statistical data. They measure attendance, converts, baptisms, programs and program strength, financial income and expenditures, building size and indebtedness, and other appropriate categories. While these are helpful, they aren't primary biblical measurements of church health. That doesn't mean they are *un*biblical, just that they are largely absent from the scriptural record. This doesn't mean they aren't helpful either. Just because something isn't explicitly in the Bible, doesn't mean it can't be a helpful part of modern church life and measuring contemporary church health.

The New Testament record doesn't include much detailed

numerical data about early churches. Attendance trends, offering amounts, building size, and any ratios of membership to church performance are omitted from the Bible. Exceptions to this are the number of converts after Peter's first message (Acts 2:41) and the apostles' early preaching in the temple (Acts 4:4). These two stories illustrate the powerful beginning of the church, but the pattern of reporting numerical gains wasn't common in Acts or the epistles. The stories of early churches, including Antioch, are told more as narratives, each one resembling a case study more than a spreadsheet.

While statistical data isn't the primary biblical means of describing church health, empirical measurements of modern church life are still helpful. Many resources exist to help you use this kind of information appropriately. This book, however, attempts to balance those valid measures by creating a process to evaluate other observable, important qualities of transformational churches. My contention is both perspectives are essential for determining the true condition of a church. Other excellent books focus on analyzing church health by quantitative data. This book is about measuring churches by the qualitative aspects modeled by the church at Antioch. Before doing that, however, let's underscore the importance of the empirical approach by considering some suggestions about how to use statistical data more effectively in measuring church health.

The Value of the Quantitative Approach

Most churches keep up with key numerical indicators of their progress. Some churches use those numbers to brag about their results, usually claiming large numbers as a leading indicator of church health. That frustrates some pastors, particularly those who have lesser numbers (but perhaps feel their church has other equally important indicators of vitality). Despite the possibility of inappropriate use, a church should keep careful record of its numerical progress and use that information as one factor in determining its overall health. Every church should grow as large as practically possible, reaching as many people with the gospel as possible and expanding its ministry influence as broadly as it can. Nothing in this book contradicts those convictions or countermands any effort to promote numerical growth. Particularly in ripe harvest fields, there is no excuse for poor numerical results. Using the qualitative approach advocated in this book to justify ineffectiveness or create a "smaller is better" mind-set is a misuse of the material.

As a pastor, and later as a church starter, we counted everything (attendance, offerings, baptisms, first-time guests, etc.) and created various matrices to analyze our progress. In the early years of our new church, for example, we even created a new attendance measurement: Monthly Cumulative Attendance (MCA). This statistic gave us a more accurate picture than weekly attendance figures of our growth as a church. It worked like this. On the first Sunday of each month, we counted the worship attendance. On the second Sunday, we counted the attendance but we also determined the "monthly cumulative attendance" for the first two Sundays, meaning the number of different people who had attended a worship service those two weeks. If the first Sunday attendance was fifty and the second Sunday attendance was also fifty (but five people attended who hadn't been present the previous week), then our MCA for the first two weeks was fifty-five. We would then continue the process for the rest of the month, tracking the people who hadn't previously attended and adding them to the MCA. At the end of each month, we charted a nonduplicating cumulative attendance for our church.

We tracked this number month by month. While weekly attendance went up and down (often dramatically as it does in most new churches), we focused on increasing our MCA every month rather than stressing about weekly attendance. If we accomplished this, it meant we were continually attracting new people who were interested enough in our church to attend a worship service. Growing the MCA told us our church was enlarging its sphere of influence, becoming known by more and more people, and maintaining its focus on continually reaching out to new people. We counted the MCA for the first few years until the weekly attendance became too large and the registration process too cumbersome to document effectively nonduplicating monthly attendance. By that time our pattern of outreach was ingrained in our congregational DNA, and the need for this kind of analysis and accountability wasn't as great.

While not all churches should use this tool, every new church should consider counting their MCA for the first few years. This number, more than fluctuating weekly attendance, reveals the growth of a church's influence and connectivity with new people— the essential lifeblood of every church plant. Suggesting another number to measure church health should remove any doubt about my valuation of empirical data and quantitative measurement of results!

There are, however, limitations to these approaches to determining church health. When church health is measured by programmatic or statistical data (like attendance, financial strength, number of baptisms, size and condition of facilities, etc.), the results can be misleading if the information isn't considered in context. For example, a small-town church may not record as many converts as a larger church in a city. The ratio of converts to the surrounding population of unconverted persons, however, may actually mean the smaller church is making a greater evangelistic impact on its area than the larger church is making. The smaller church may also have a greater ratio of new converts to its existing members, indicating it may be, in some ways more evangelistically effective than the larger church. The question of measuring evangelistic effectiveness isn't as simple as counting the converts or baptisms. An honest appraisal of your church's health evaluates your results in context, not just the raw data.

One church in a timber-industry community on the Oregon coast illustrates this point. The town once had five lumber mills. One by one, over the years, they all went out of business. When the last mill closed, the church lost sixty-seven members in one year who relocated to find employment in other places. Yet, while this church lost a significant number of its members, it managed to reach enough people to keep its attendance even with the previous year. By most denominational definitions, this church was a "plateaued" church—same attendance year-by-year. Not so! This was actually a growing, relatively healthy church. Numbers are important in evaluating a church's condition but only in the proper context. It takes spiritually perceptive leaders to evaluate their church by considering the data in context, rather than simply celebrating having "more" than other churches may have or than they had the previous year.

Another church reported more than six hundred converts through its ministry in a five-year time frame. This happened in a county with a population of about ten thousand. If conversions happened at the same ratio in San Jose, California (population one million), sixty thousand conversions would have been registered! When the context is considered, a church reaching six hundred new converts in a small county is making a greater impact in its area than a church reaching the same number of people in a large city. Context matters!

The Value of Qualitative Analysis

Empirical data, even when viewed in context, isn't enough to determine a church's true status. Subjective analysis, using what is sometimes called "soft data" must also be considered to determine the spiritual vitality of a congregation. Both quantitative and qualitative analyses are essential to create a true picture of a church's condition. These are complementary but different ways to evaluate performance. They require a different rubric, a different grading scale for evaluation.

To help you understand the difference in these two approaches, consider an academic example. Objective facts, "hard data," might be used as the grading scale to determine the grade a student receives in a course. Points would be earned for excellent papers, high test scores, and perfect attendance—an "A" student, to be sure! But suppose you asked another set of questions. What if you asked: "Did the student's life change as a result of these assignments? Is there evidence the information learned resulted in life transformation?" That requires a different set of measurements, a different way to gather results before reaching ultimate and accurate conclusions. Suppose the course required the student to memorize a definition of *compassion* and outline a biblical example of Jesus demonstrating compassion. Grading those results would be relatively easy. What if, instead of simply measuring the student's ability to memorize and recall data, you evaluated instances the student demonstrated compassion in interpersonal relationships? Measuring that requires a different method of gathering information about the student's learning outcomes and a completely different grading system.

Now apply this to a church example: measuring the growth of the missional commitment of teenagers in your youth group. One way to demonstrate growth would be counting the attendance at training events or the number of students who volunteer for a summer mission project. If these are increasing annually, it may be a positive indicator of a growing awareness of missional responsibility. But it might also mean the boys wanted more time with their girlfriends or more parents were willing to pay for a trip since it was less expensive than the trip the previous summer. Attendance at training events or on mission trips should be counted and considered but may not tell the whole story. Suppose you also observed significantly more prayer for missionaries by these teenagers, or self-initiated service to raise money for mission projects, or some former teenagers making vocational commitments to missionary service as young adults. These subjective, though observable phenomenon, are also indicators of a growing commitment to missions. Coupled with improved attendance, they would indicate spiritual growth among your teenagers. Even paired with lesser attendance, they might still indicate some growth in the missional commitment of your youth group.

A subjective approach to measuring church health can be more difficult because it is based more on observation (and spiritual discernment) than simply counting numbers. It can lead to overly optimistic conclusions when leaders are unwilling to evaluate critically their work and the condition of their church. A subjective approach can easily be manipulated (but then so can statistics and program data). A subjective approach asks tough questions, some of which are included at the end of each of the following chapters, and answers them honestly. This kind of evaluation, since it's subjective, can also lead driven church leaders to be hypercritical. Asking hard questions shouldn't always lead to negative answers. Be careful not to assume everyone must somehow come up short in this kind of process. It's possible to celebrate partial success while also acknowledging need for improvement.

Throughout this book, you will be challenged to analyze the subjective qualities of church health in your context. It may be easy to read through the next seven chapters quickly, checking qualities off one by one and claiming your church is healthy because there is some evidence of each of them in your fellowship. Be more congregationally aware and self-critical than that. Analyze each of these qualities in your context. Determine the true health of your church, not the level of health you wish for it. Be willing to make the hard choices to confront weakness and blind spots. Beware the self-deception that occurs when we compare ourselves to the church down the street or to what our church did last year as the primary measures of our effectiveness.

One well-respected pastor leads a larger church that appears healthy. He knows better. While it appears to be a model to outsiders, he knows the inside story. When considered in its context and compared to its potential, the church's impact is actually diminishing annually. The church has lost its entrepreneurial edge, seldom experiences the Holy Spirit's power in fresh ways, and is spending a greater percentage of its resources on itself year by year. His experience of confronting the church with his appraisal has been frustrating. They *feel* healthy, they *appear* successful, and outsiders *admire* them so their response to his entreaties has been predictably slow. Like the boy in *The Emperor's New Clothes*, he points out the church's spiritual nakedness while everyone else admires its invisible clothing! Like the little boy in the story, he is discovering some people prefer living an illusion to confronting reality.

Leaders define reality. That can be a lonely role. While others can afford the luxury of self-deception, leaders can't. This doesn't mean leaders only see the negative side of things. Critical appraisal doesn't equate to negative appraisal. It means honest evaluation, a precursor to real change. If you are a church leader, this is your responsibility. You can't shirk it or delegate it to someone else. Courageously face reality.

The Antioch Case: Strengths and Limitations

Considering the story of Antioch—its nuances, settings, and implications—provides a mother lode to mine for principles and patterns of healthy church life. This book extracts from this biblical case study some qualities describing and defining a transformational church. Since you have probably glanced at the table of contents, you know the core of this book is seven qualities that mark a transformational church. Why seven? Could it have been five or eight or twelve? Sure. Some of the principles identified here could be grouped differently. There may also be additional subsets to these seven qualities. A supporting theme might be prioritized, thus creating a longer list. A case study approach of any situation is always somewhat arbitrary.

My intent isn't to advocate for an absolute list. My goal is to describe and categorize principles emerging from careful consideration of a biblical model. These seven qualities are just hangers on which the discussion can be displayed. These qualities, while emerging from a biblical model, also resonate with me as practically applicable after more than thirty years of church leadership and training church leaders. They are as true for the church today and tomorrow as they were in Antioch.

Another significant qualifier for these attributes is they

are essential no matter the culture, location, size, resources, or nationality of the church. Too often, standards of church health are created based on a particular church methodology, culture, or background. This can be helpful but only when analyzing a church in a similar setting. If we aren't careful, we can fall into the trap of equating "transformational church" with "church the way we do it." For example, one pastor forcefully preached his conviction that a well-trained, generously funded staff of ministers was required to create a healthy church in North America. His audience—mostly bivocational pastors and church planters—was not convinced his middle-class, suburban methodology was really required to build a strong church. Similarly, another speaker embarrassed himself by demanding certain qualities of church life as essential, not realizing his particular methodology was offensive to Asian pastors in his audience. A professor lectured on the proper style of preaching in healthy churches, only to be humbled when African students contested his cultural bias by reminding him of their effectiveness with a different approach. Unfortunately, while I only saw the first two mistakes, I was guilty of the third one! Cultural bias afflicts us all and colors what we believe about church life.

The church at Antioch was birthed in a specific context, but the qualities emerging from this study are transcultural, not limited to Antioch. Church health must be measured by analyzing universal principles, not just critiquing success at implementing culturally determined methodologies. For example, as we will see in chapter 7, managing conflict effectively is a mark of a transformational church. While that is universally true, how conflict is managed appropriately is strongly conditioned by culture. We are constantly faced with the challenge, as biblical interpreters, to ferret universally true principles out of the culturally influenced first-century record. To facilitate this requires a transcultural assessment of qualities appropriate in every setting without getting lost in the maze of current methodological diversity. While this book attempts to do this, let me apologize now for the shortcomings revealed by my cultural myopia and unintentional biases.

This book will give you tools to consider your church from a new perspective. You will learn to look at the spiritual, relational, doctrinal, and attitudinal qualities defining a healthy church. From those descriptors, a portrait of transformational church will emerge. In working through this process, you will be challenged to make subjective appraisals of relative strength in your setting. For most of these qualities, the "grade" will be on a continuum of progress. In other words, progress is marked by gradations of success that are ever-evolving, like the bars on a cell phone or a meter with a 1 to 10 scale. As you will discover, the qualities of church health modeled by Antioch aren't characteristics a church either has or doesn't have. These are qualities most churches have *to some degree.* The challenge for you, as a leader, is to determine honestly, in your context, your church's relative condition in each area and then *move the needle on the meter in the right direction!* Doing so will help your church become more transformational—a church that changes individuals, shapes communities, and impacts our world.

Questions for Reflection

1. Do you have accurate statistical data to measure your church's health? How are you currently using this information? How can you improve your use of it? Do you need any further statistical data to assist your analysis? How will you gather it?

2. Are you currently using any subjective data to evaluate your church's health? How effective has this been? Do you believe you have an accurate picture of your church's health at this time? If not, what areas need further investigation?

3. What concerns do you have about using "soft data" to determine church health? Are you open to the potential benefits of such information?

4. Has measuring church health, formally or informally, been used to harm you or your church in the past? If so, how? As you make this study, how will you avoid those mistakes and work toward more helpful outcomes?

5. What cultural biases impact the analysis of your church? How can you develop a larger worldview so your analysis isn't constrained by your perspective or the perspectives of your church's members?

Part 2

A Picture of a
Transformational Church

Chapter 3

Spiritual Power

A transformational church is empowered
by the Holy Spirit.

The church at Antioch was empowered by the Holy Spirit. In our day of complex church programs created and managed by professionally trained ministers, advocating dependence on the Spirit to empower the church sounds anachronistic and outdated. Words like *anointing, unction,* and *filling* aren't common descriptors of church leaders or church ministries. Few conferences promoting ministerial leadership methods prioritize experiencing the Holy Spirit. When we analyze a leader's resume, we usually look more for educational achievements and ministerial accomplishments than for evidence of spiritual power. We often measure churches the same way, focusing on external accoutrements like buildings or programs rather than considering spiritual depth.

Both personal and corporate successes can be Spirit empowered, and let's hope they are! They can also result from concentrated human effort. It takes spiritual discernment and disciplined thinking to know the difference between fleshly competence and spiritual power. A transformational church is empowered by the

Holy Spirit. An empowered church requires Spirit-filled leaders. Courageous leaders won't settle for less, personally or corporately.

The Holy Spirit in Antioch

There are three specific references to the Holy Spirit in the story of the church at Antioch, as well as many implied references since the book of Acts is more the Acts of the *Holy Spirit* than the Acts of the *Apostles*. The first direct reference is the description of Barnabas as "full of the Holy Spirit" (Acts 11:24). The second reference is to Agabus, a prophet from Jerusalem, predicting "by the Spirit" (Acts 11:28) that a famine was coming. The third is to the Holy Spirit intervening in a worship service to call Paul and Barnabas to missionary service (Acts 13:2).

The work of the Spirit is also implied throughout the Antioch narrative. For example, the Spirit no doubt superintended the preachers who boldly planted the gospel and the church among the Gentile community in Antioch. The Spirit certainly sustained the church's continued support for mission work as it developed over the years. The absence of the words "Holy Spirit" from a story in the text doesn't mean the Spirit wasn't involved. For the sake of clarity and specificity, however, this chapter will focus on the explicit references to the Spirit in the biblical record of Antioch. First, let's consider the role of the Spirit in and among church leaders. Then, let's consider the role of the Spirit in the church, particularly as it meets in public worship.

The Holy Spirit Fills Leaders

Barnabas was originally sent from Jerusalem, in an apostolic role, to investigate the report of Gentiles becoming Christians in Antioch without first becoming Jews. The Jerusalem church was a Jewish church, and many of its leaders were convinced conversion to Christianity came with or after becoming a Jew. This controversy would later erupt in a full-blown conflict leading to the Jerusalem Council (Acts 15).

After Barnabas arrived in Antioch, his appraisal of the situation differed from the presumption of those who dispatched him from Jerusalem. Barnabas surveyed the situation, validated what was happening, and concluded Gentiles really could become Christians without first becoming Jews. When Barnabas "arrived and saw the grace of God, he was glad, and he encouraged all of them to remain true to the Lord with a firm resolve of the heart" (Acts 11:23). He later brought Saul (Paul) from Tarsus (Acts 11:25). The two of them went to work making disciples and bringing structure to the developing church.

Barnabas was described as "a good man, full of the Holy Spirit and of faith" (Acts 11:24). Although Barnabas came from Jerusalem in an apostolic role, he quickly assumed a pastoral role in Antioch. The church at Antioch, then, identified its earliest and most prominent leader as being filled with the Holy Spirit.

For a church to experience the power of the Holy Spirit, it must have leaders who are filled with the Spirit. To be filled with the Spirit means to be controlled by the Spirit, to be under His guiding influence. It means your will is submitted to the Spirit's leadership. You are no longer independent or self-reliant—no longer trusting your strength, judgment, intellect, or training. A person filled with the Holy Spirit has emptied himself, emulating Jesus in "assuming the form of a slave" (Phil. 2:7), becoming a servant of the Spirit's desires, impulses, and urges. A Spirit-filled leader is empowered by the Spirit, producing spiritual fruit and supernatural results.

The significance of Spirit-filled leaders can't be overstated. It's essential because no church's spiritual vitality will ever rise *to stay* above the spiritual devotion and maturity of its leaders. While an occasional spurt of spiritual growth is possible—like while hosting a guest speaker, during a special worship service, or perhaps on a leadership retreat—no church's spiritual power will exceed, over time, that of its leaders. The spiritual responsibility to be a pacesetter is a normal expectation of pastoral leaders. Pastors, and others in related ministerial roles, are *spiritual* leaders. We aren't primarily organizers or administrators. Our leadership skills are more than a collection of abilities and acquired techniques. We are more than speakers and motivators influencing people by charisma or intellect. We are spiritual leaders. We model what it means to follow the Spirit's leading, to be Spirit-controlled, to be in biblical language, "filled with the Spirit."

How, then, is a person filled with the Holy Spirit? While being filled with the Spirit is mentioned several times in Acts and commanded in Ephesians 5:18, no biblical formula guarantees the experience. For example, believers were filled with the Spirit when the church was inaugurated (Acts 2:4); Peter was filled while preaching (Acts 4:8); the church was filled during a prayer meeting (Acts 4:31); Stephen was filled at his martyrdom trial (Acts 7:55); Paul was filled as part of Ananias's visit (Acts 9:17); Paul was filled while confronting a sorcerer (Acts 13:9); and the Pisidian Antioch church (the *other* Antioch) was filled in the midst of both blessing and persecution (Acts 13:52). While these fillings are reported, the process of how they happened is omitted. This was intentional (in God's wisdom) to prevent formulaic incantations developing as a false means to pseudo-spiritual power. In short, there's no mantra to chant or script to memorize that guarantees a Spirit-filled life.

In every case in the Bible, the result of the Spirit's filling is emphasized more than the process of filling. Examples of these results include: the church spoke the gospel in various languages (Acts 2:4); Peter preached courageously (Acts 4:8–22); the church witnessed with boldness (Acts 4:31); Stephen was sustained through his death (Acts 7:56–60); Paul was delivered from blindness (Acts 9:18); a sorcerer was blinded and a proconsul believed (Acts 13:11–12); and the church experienced joy in the midst of hardship (Acts 13:52). What can be learned from this pattern?

The most important insight is this: While there is no formula for being filled with the Spirit, *the results of being filled are vital.* Because of this, it behooves us to try to answer the question, "How is a person filled with the Spirit?" While there is no formula, principles can be discerned from various biblical passages to facilitate this process. As part of understanding the work of the Spirit, the following aspects of being filled must be considered. The choice of "aspects" to describe this list is intentional. The following are aspects of being filled with the Spirit, not *steps* to being filled. Experiencing the Holy Spirit can't be reduced to a series of steps. Experiencing the Spirit isn't an assembly process like putting prayer A in time slot Z! A dynamic relationship with God defies such arbitrary categorization. Nevertheless, we aren't without biblical direction guiding us toward the Spirit's filling.

The first aspect of being filled with the Holy Spirit is conversion. All believers "led by God's Spirit are God's sons. For you did not receive a spirit of slavery to fall back into fear, but you received the Spirit of adoption, by whom we cry out, 'Abba, Father!' The Spirit Himself testifies together with our spirit that we are God's children" (Rom. 8:14–16). As a believer, at your conversion you received the Holy Spirit as a permanent, indwelling presence that lasts a lifetime. Being filled with the Spirit isn't receiving something new. It's unleashing the influence of Someone who is already a core part of your spiritual existence.

The second aspect of being filled with the Spirit is surrendering control of your life. Many years ago a deacon told me being filled with the Spirit required "acquiescence of the heart to God." *Acquiescence* was a new word for me! It means "passive submission, willing compliance." No other word, in more than thirty years of searching, better sums up this aspect of being filled with the Spirit. Besides, the word just sounds so spiritual! Being filled with the Spirit involves surrendering control of your life to the Holy Spirit. It's a willing choice to become passive, to submit, to willingly cede control to the Spirit's influence.

Fresh submission can be experienced through regular transparent prayer, not perfunctory or habitual prayers mouthed mindlessly. Bowing your head, getting down on your knees, or lying on the ground and asking the Spirit to control your life can symbolize submission. When you humble yourself, you admit your lack of human-generated power (or wisdom, or ability, or anything else that smacks of adequacy), and put yourself on the path to spiritual power. Prayer crystallizes submission. But rote, formulaic praying is insufficient. Crying out to God—earnestly, passionately abandoning all pretenses—is praying that genuinely reveals lack of self-trust and a longing for the Spirit's filling.

This doesn't imply the effort in your prayers makes them more efficacious. Describing earnest prayer as the means to adequately express your submission to God doesn't mean there's magic in bowing, kneeling, or otherwise expressing yourself. No outer work, no matter how earnest, produces spiritual change. The issue is *acquiescence* of your heart, not any certain method or mode of prayer. Outward expressions can be helpful in expressing our innermost desires. They can also facilitate humbling ourselves, assuring God's favor because He "resists the proud, but gives grace to the humble" (1 Pet. 5:5). But no outer work accomplishes inner surrender. That's accomplished by choosing to submit your will to God.

A third aspect of being filled with the Spirit is stopping sinful behavior. Since the Holy Spirit entered your life at conversion, being filled with the Spirit is more about removing barriers to His flow through you than obtaining something new. This idea is captured in the simple phrase, "Don't stifle the Spirit" (1 Thess. 5:19). Other translations use the word *quench*. Either word communicates the same idea. The Holy Spirit is alive in you. Yet you have the capacity to stifle or quench His influence. How? The context of this warning encourages believers to maintain spiritual disciplines like prayer and responding to prophetic (or preached) messages. You quench the Spirit when you neglect spiritual disciplines like prayer, Bible reading, and worship attendance.

The Holy Spirit's power can also be limited by your attitudes or actions. In the midst of instructions about proper behavior for believers, Paul wrote, "And don't grieve God's Holy Spirit" (Eph. 4:30). That admonition is in the midst of instructions about managing anger, showing integrity at work, communicating with wholesome words, and avoiding bitterness, wrath, and slander. The context of the warning is significant. You can grieve the Holy Spirit by your actions and attitudes. Your actions reveal who is controlling you. Your attitudes show what shapes your thinking. When you are in control, your attitudes and actions drift toward self-serving, self-justifying behavior unseemly for believers. These actions reveal you aren't submitted to the Spirit; therefore, not filled with the Spirit. Your actions, and the attitudes motivating those actions, are a barometer on your spiritual condition.

A final aspect of being filled by the Holy Spirit is accepting His filling by faith. When you pray—confessing known sin, submitting yourself to the Spirit's control, and asking for the filling of the Spirit—no special feeling will necessarily wash over you. Giving control to the Spirit is a spiritual exercise accomplished by faith. Remember, "as you have received Christ Jesus the Lord, walk in Him" (Col. 2:6). You received Jesus into your life by faith. In that moment the Holy Spirit permanently indwelled you. Submitting yourself to the Spirit's control is a continuing act of faith. Believing you have His power, and acting upon it, is a faith-filled choice.

While the focus on the Spirit in Acts isn't about revealing a formula for being filled, there is a clear record of the results of His filling. Barnabas's being filled with the Spirit was one of the reasons "large numbers of people were added to the Lord" (Acts 11:24). Barnabas's assignment for missionary service was a result of the Holy Spirit's intervention in a worship service (Acts 13:2). Clearly Barnabas models supernatural results and receiving life direction through the power of the Spirit.

Other results in other settings in Acts included preaching boldly, courageously, and in various languages (Acts 2:4; 4:8–22, 31; 7:2–60), blindness inflicted and relieved (Acts 13:11–12; 9:18), and joy in the midst of persecution and suffering (Acts 13:52). These results might be grouped in two broad categories—spiritual fruit (like joy) and supernatural results (like healings and conversions). These, then, are the two primary marks of the filling of the Spirit in church leaders, spiritual fruit and supernatural results.

The fruit of the Spirit (Gal. 5:22–23—love, joy, peace, patience, kindness, goodness, faith, gentleness, and self-control) are character qualities produced by the Spirit. These aren't native to humanity or produced by natural effort. They certainly aren't common qualities valued among worldly leaders—just check out the "business leadership" section of any bookstore. Yet these are precisely the qualities the Spirit produces and expects Christian leaders to exemplify.

When ministry leaders are filled with the Spirit, their character development reveals spiritual growth or spiritual fruit. Christian leaders are role models. Their leadership competency is actually defined more by character than skill. For example, the qualities outlined in 1 Timothy 3:2–7 are heavily tilted toward character issues over performance capabilities. A pastoral leader must have some skills like being able to teach and to manage "his own household competently" (1 Tim. 3:2, 4). But the other ten to twelve traits in this passage (depending on how they are grouped) are all character qualities.

Clearly then, one aspect of being Spirit filled is demonstrating transformed character—change produced by the Holy Spirit shaping your mind, will, and emotions so you demonstrate being "a new creation" (2 Cor. 5:17) in Jesus. The label "fruit" communicates something passively produced by the natural process of a source expressing itself. Jesus said, "I am the vine; you are the branches. The one who remains in Me and I in him produces much fruit, because you can do nothing without Me" (John 15:5). Jesus, in you as the indwelling Holy Spirit, is your Source for spiritual fruit. Character transformation, unexplainable except as the result of transformation by Jesus, is evidence of the Spirit's filling. Healthy churches have transforming leaders whose lives bear spiritual fruit.

The other evidence of the Spirit's filling is supernatural ministry results. These may take many forms, but the results most closely associated with Barnabas at Antioch were large numbers of converts and the missionary advance of the gospel. Under Barnabas's leadership "large numbers of people were added to the Lord" (Acts 11:24). While Barnabas was teamed with Paul, the gospel advanced to new cities and territories with large numbers of people becoming believers (Acts 13–14). Barnabas was winsome, a leader with demonstrated effectiveness in winning people to faith in Jesus Christ.

Some leaders are more gifted evangelists than others. Being filled with the Spirit doesn't mean you will reach as many people as Billy Graham or Rick Warren. But it means you will have *some* effectiveness in communicating the gospel and facilitating conversion. Leaders set the pace in reaching people for Christ. We are uniquely responsible to help the church stay focused on its primary mission of sharing the gospel. A person being saved through your witness is a supernatural result. If no one is ever converted through your work, it's fair to question your filling by the Holy Spirit. The filling of the Spirit produces various supernatural results including the miracle of conversions happening through your preaching, teaching, sharing, and/or modeling the gospel.

When is the last time you shared the gospel? Preached a gospel-centered message? Engaged in a meaningful gospel conversation with an unbeliever? Were present when a person made a commitment to Jesus as Savior and Lord? When was the last time a conversion movement happened through your ministry? A mission team or new church plant was launched from your church? If your answer to these questions reveals a lack of evangelistic fervor, you may not be filled with the Holy Spirit. Supernatural results like conversions are one indicator of the Spirit's filling of a church leader. While there are other indicators, this one was the focus in Antioch and should be a primary focus for us as well.

The Holy Spirit in the Church

The first reference to the Holy Spirit in Antioch was describing Barnabas. The other two references are in the context of worship services. The first of these describes Agabus who "predicted by the Spirit" (Acts 11:28) that a severe famine was coming. The second reference was to the Spirit's direction in a worship service resulting in Barnabas and Paul's being dispatched as the first missionary team. Let's look at each of these incidents more closely.

Agabus was a speaker of some renown from the Jerusalem church (Acts 21:10) who came to Antioch to preach. On the surface that doesn't seem too remarkable. Barnabas had already come from Jerusalem and established himself as a leader in Antioch. The Jerusalem church was the "mother church" of the early Christian movement. It would be natural for one of its leaders to preach in Antioch, particularly if he had a Spirit-prompted, special prophetic message to deliver. Agabus predicted a famine which happened "during the time of Claudius" (Acts 11:28).

The response of the Antioch believers is, again on the surface, what might be expected. They heard their brothers and sisters in Jerusalem would soon be suffering, so they collected an offering and sent Barnabas and Paul to deliver it. It was a relief offering, an act of love from one church family to another. That all seems normal until you consider the backstory of the relationship between these two churches.

The launch of the Antioch church had been scandalous to the Jerusalem church. Imagine—Gentiles becoming Christians without first becoming Jews! The Jerusalem church was a Jewish movement. Jesus told them to take the gospel to the entire world, but they kept it in the Jerusalem area for many years. It took the persecution of Stephen to cause the Christian Diaspora, scattering the church and initiating a broad gospel movement among Gentiles in Antioch. When this news reached Jerusalem, Barnabas was dispatched to investigate (and some hoped terminate) the fledging heresy that had created the supposed pseudo-church in Antioch.

The depth of feeling on these matters is later shown by the intensity of deliberations at the Jerusalem Council (Acts 15). Barnabas, however, discerned the legitimacy of the Spirit's work in creating the new church. Rather than stymie the effort, he remained in Antioch and facilitated the church's development.

Against that backdrop, consider afresh the response of the Antioch Christians to Agabus. A leader from a church that hoarded the gospel and questioned their legitimacy had the audacity to ask the Antioch believers for an offering! Remarkably, they gave it generously, sacrificially, and without reservation.

This story reveals two aspects of the Spirit's work in the worship services at Antioch. First, the Spirit enabled preaching by Agabus and receptivity among the congregation. Second, the Spirit enabled generous giving. Keep those two aspects in mind as we consider other ways the Spirit worked in a subsequent worship service in Antioch.

Time passed, and several men—Barnabas, Simeon, Lucius, Manaen, and Paul—emerged as a leadership team for the Antioch church. They were directing a worship service that involved prayer and fasting when one or more of them (or perhaps other members) was prompted with an unusual message: "The Holy Spirit said, 'Set apart for Me Barnabas and Saul [Paul] for the work that I have called them to'" (Acts 13:2). After hearing the message, they "fasted, prayed, and laid hands on them, [and] they sent them off" (Acts 13:3).

These events were unusual for at least three reasons. First, the message came *through* the church *to* the missionary team. Most often, when God gives a directive, He gives it directly to the recipient. Not this time. He spoke through others to call Barnabas and Paul to leave Antioch as missionaries. Second, this was unusual because it had never happened before. While the mission imperative was established by Jesus (Acts 1:8), the Jerusalem church was slow to develop an intentional strategy for kingdom advance. This is the first time a church formally set apart workers and sent them on a mission trip. And third, these circumstances were unusual because the most senior leaders left the church, unlike Jerusalem where the apostles remained while others scattered (Acts 8:1). Most of the time, then and now, senior leaders facilitate others' answering God's missionary call. This time the process was reversed. The church told its senior leaders, their most respected leaders, God wanted them to leave.

The Holy Spirit was active in the worship services at Antioch. The Spirit empowered the preachers. He enabled congregational response to their sermons. He motivated a generous offering. The Spirit directed the congregation with a message for its leaders. He called ministry leaders to new responsibilities including leaving pastoral leadership for itinerant ministry. These patterns are still evidence of the Spirit's work in worship gatherings today.

The Holy Spirit still empowers speakers and energizes the preached Word of God. He still enables congregational response, including generous giving. The Spirit directs congregational decision-making, calls people to new fields of service, and sustains missionary advance by motivating churches to give up their assets—people (the missionary team) and money (the relief offering)—for kingdom advance.

Transformational churches experience the power of the Holy Spirit in their worship services. They have *a holy expectation* something will happen *every time* they gather to worship God. These churches have leaders and members who seek God's power in planning, preparing for, and directing worship services. Transformational churches experience the Spirit's intervention while worshipping.

How can you discern if the Holy Spirit is moving in the worship services of your church? Simply put, supernatural events happen. Decisions are made and life change happens beyond the scope of human ingenuity. People give gifts, make commitments, and chart new directions because of insight received while worshipping. In short, things happen that can't be explained by the work of your two hands.

One church was fund-raising for a major building project. Experts predicted the church would raise three times its annual budget over a three-year time frame in special offerings for the building, a maximum of about one million dollars. On commitment day the lay couple directing the campaign outlined their process of deciding to make a significant gift. They told their story of saving, through thick and thin, for the honeymoon they never had—a trip to Australia. They had accumulated the money and planned to take the trip on their twenty-fifth wedding anniversary the following summer. Instead, they announced they had given their trip savings to the building fund. Their story, their sacrifice, and the transparency of their motives were like an electrical current pulsating through the congregation. A spirit of giving, orchestrated by no one but prompted by the Holy Spirit, took over. The church committed to give more than two million dollars that day and fulfilled those commitments over the next three years. It was a supernatural offering by a church of about 250 people.

Another church created an opportunity for immediate response, through baptism, in a worship service. Rather than preach on baptism and ask people to be baptized later at a more convenient date, the pastor preached on baptism and called for immediate response. In three worship services, attended by about five hundred people, 109 people were baptized. Some left the first service, called friends and family members, and came back to the next service to be baptized. Then some of those guests were converted and immediately baptized. Supernatural results and some dirty water by the end of the day!

While preaching, a speaker reported, "It felt like I was being carried along while I preached. It was almost as if I were standing on the side watching myself. The congregation's attentiveness was extremely unusual." At the end, dozens responded publicly to his call for holy living, and several committed themselves to ministry leadership. Another pastor said, "The applications people made of my message astounded me. God was at work to confront and change people on issues I was completely unaware they were facing." These are supernatural results, for the preacher and the listener, as the Holy Spirit works in worship services.

One of the casualties of some contemporary worship styles has been the loss of a call for public responses in worship services. Many churches have moved away from calling for public decisions to avoid embarrassing people or putting them on the spot. While that seems like an admirable goal, it can undercut the opportunity for people to respond to the Spirit's prompting in worship. When the Holy Spirit moved in the church at Antioch, the members *did something.*

They responded to preaching, gave money, delivered messages to fellow believers, accepted a call to missions, fasted, prayed, and laid hands on fellow believers (commissioning them for service).

When the Holy Spirit is active in a worship service, people respond—privately yes, but also openly, definitively, and publicly. Certainly this can be manipulated and be too dependent on emotional appeals. But foregoing all opportunity for public response in worship isn't the answer to those excesses. Leading worship services with integrity, including having the courage to stop pointless emotional displays that detract from worship in the name of "following the Spirit," is part of effective church leadership.

Transformational churches and their leaders have a sense of expectancy when they gather for worship. They seek the filling of the Spirit personally and the empowering of the Spirit corporately. These churches create space—spiritual, emotional, and physical— for people to respond to the Spirit's prompting in worship. They facilitate praying, sharing testimonies, confronting sinful behavior, public repentance and supportive prayer, and expressions of mutual support (laying on hands in Antioch, often a hug or handshake today). These churches plan time in their worship services for response using various methods but always giving people an opportunity to follow the Spirit's promptings, urgings, or instructions. Transformational churches expect the Holy Spirit to be an active participant when they worship.

When the Spirit is conspicuously inactive, healthy churches remove known barriers to His work. Churches, like individuals, can quench the Spirit by their attitudes and behaviors. One congregation had bitter conflict in a church meeting. For months following, no spiritual responses were evident in the worship services. Finally, after the leaders facilitated public repentance, confession, and restoration of relationships, the Spirit once again began moving in their midst. For six months there had been no public professions of faith in Jesus. On the night of the church's repentance/healing service, a first-time guest was converted during the response time. Healthy churches remove barriers to experiencing the Holy Spirit while worshipping.

Transformational churches are empowered by the Spirit and have Spirit-filled leaders. When the Holy Spirit is actively working in a church and its leaders, spiritual fruit and supernatural results are evident. This doesn't mean every person has a dramatic, life-altering experience in every worship service. It does mean, though, these kinds of experiences are happening regularly and in ways that can't be predicted or controlled. A transformational church has serendipitous experiences with the Holy Spirit. Be honest about your church and about yourself as you reflect on the Spirit's role in your life and the work of your church.

Questions for Reflection

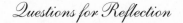

1. Are you filled with the Spirit? Are you experiencing spiritual fruit and supernatural results in your ministry? If not, what will you do about it?

2. Is your church empowered by the Spirit? Do your people experience life change in or because of your worship services? What is happening in your church that can't be explained by human effort or ingenuity?

3. Are you substituting worldly measures of strength—like reputation, building size, budget surplus, or inflated membership numbers—for a genuine appraisal of your church's spiritual health?

4. Is there evidence, spiritual fruit and supernatural results, of the Holy Spirit's work through your church in your

community? Are unbelievers being converted? Are believers being transformed?

5. On a scale of 1 to 10, how would you rate your church's current experience of the Holy Spirit? What can you do to move the meter to a higher number?

Chapter 4

An Entrepreneurial Mind-Set

A transformational church innovates
to advance the gospel.

❖ Openness to innovation, which often leads to significant change, is required to sustain a transformational church. That's troubling news for some Christians who don't like change and don't want to hear any proposals about innovating new forms of ministry. Many well-meaning believers want their church to remain just as it is. A person usually joins a church for the church it *is*, not the church someone else envisions it becoming. When a church begins to change or even when pastoral leaders start talking about making significant changes, the comfort level among the membership usually declines. Consequently, the anxiety level for leaders often soars. Innovation and change can be unsettling for everyone. While a healthy sense of stability contributes to emotional equilibrium, both personally and corporately, rigid resistance to change is counterproductive to growth. Healthy organisms, including churches, are either growing and changing or dying.

Leaders are change agents. It's in our DNA, a core part of our role and responsibility. We resist the status quo and welcome new initiatives. Learning to lead *healthy* change, not just change for change's sake, is our challenge. Some leaders are poor change managers. They introduce unnecessary change using inappropriate methods for uncertain purposes. These changes are counterproductive to church health, often doing more harm than good. Without a doubt leaders need to develop and improve their change-management skill set.

Sometimes, however, the problem isn't the leader. It's the followers. Some Christians resist even simple changes, much less major innovations, adamantly rejecting all proposals for anything new. In those cases the problem isn't lack of skill in presenting a change. It's a much deeper spiritual problem. When it comes to experiencing change, both leaders and followers need to avoid the common mistakes that undermine this process. Learning to manage change effectively, to be transformed in healthy way, is foundational to building a healthy church.

Common Mistakes

The first mistake is introducing change for the wrong reasons, which are many and varied. Some of the wrong motives for introducing change include wanting to make the church more comfortable (physically or spiritually) for its members, making the church like the pastor's last church (so it's easier for him to manage), changing aspects of a church's function largely irrelevant to accomplishing its mission (making major issues out of minor problems), and changing to copy some successful church somewhere (discovered in the last conference the pastor attended). Church members can also initiate or demand change for similar reasons. Either way, poor motives for change produce unhealthy results even when the change is implemented successfully.

Another mistake is changing too frequently—haphazard,

hurried change in the absence of a compelling reason for urgency. Some leaders enjoy the adrenaline rush of creating pseudo-emergencies seemingly justifying a rapid response. This ultimately creates change aversion or resistance among followers. Christians become discouraged by unnecessary or unhelpful changes thrust on them by well-intentioned leaders trying to keep up with the church down the street or to satisfy their own ego needs. Believers can be worn out from trying to keep up with passing fads and frustrated with their leader's addiction to a frantic pace of change management.

Change that doesn't produce intended results can also be destructive. When a church changes, it should do so to improve its missional effectiveness. Some leaders promise these results to motivate followers to adopt their recommendations. When the results fail to materialize, those same leaders are reluctant to admit their mistake and redirect the church's energies to more productive pursuits. When new ideas have poor results, capable leaders admit the truth and move on. In short, when the horse dies, dismount!

When other pastors asked me how our church plant grew, it always disappointed me they didn't want to hear our failure stories. Our failures were often significant because they pointed us to our successes. We tried many strategies, some complete failures, as we struggled to expand our witness and lead more people to Jesus. Our church's entrepreneurial mind-set, a willingness to try new idea after new idea, was strengthened by our corresponding willingness to admit when something wasn't working and move on. We learned from trial and error what worked and what didn't. We also learned to fail fast and move on to more productive efforts.

Another common problem is leaders introducing self-serving change masked as a means of church improvement. One pastor attended a church growth conference in a distant state and became convinced his church was out of touch with its community. He determined to implement culturally relevant evangelism strategies (actually only copying what was relevant to the distant church, not his location). He went back home and changed everything. Over the next few years, the church shrunk from an attendance close to eight hundred to just over two hundred. All the while, the pastor kept pressing for more radical changes so they would "reach their community." This pastor was deceived, driven more by his need to lead a certain style church than to connect with his community. He eventually resigned, satisfied he had done his job well in leading the church to change while ignoring the sad reality of the lost membership and the church's diminished evangelistic footprint.

While these are some wrong reasons to change, do *not* conclude all change at church is bad. The opposite is true! An entrepreneurial mind-set, a willingness to innovate and change, is essential for church health. This mind-set embraces change as a desirable part of church life. When a church has an entrepreneurial mind-set, their default answer to suggestions of new approaches or methods is, "Yes, let's consider it." They may not adopt every proposal, but their attitude embraces the possibility of change when an opportunity is presented.

Leaders of these churches know the best reason to introduce change to a church: to better fulfill the mission of getting the gospel to as many people as possible in the shortest time possible. Every new idea must be measured by that standard. Any other motive or anticipated outcome for change can become personally self-serving or congregationally self-preserving. The mission of the church is enlarging the impact of the gospel. Change—sometimes radical, painful change to accomplish that purpose—is essential. Change for any other reason can be a devilish distraction. Toward that end, innovating to advance the gospel, let's look back to Antioch as an example of a transformational church, positively experiencing change and producing changed lives.

Innovations at Antioch

The church at Antioch modeled a series of firsts among churches. They were *First* Church, Antioch in numerous ways, each directly connected to the mission of advancing the gospel. The mission of the Antioch church, as well as the church today, can be expressed with one or more relatively synonymous phrases: sharing the gospel, expanding the kingdom, enlarging the church, being missional, being on mission, advancing the gospel, etc. However it's stated, the driving passion for the church at Antioch was reaching unbelievers with the good news of Jesus. Transformational churches have this same mission today. Zeal for accomplishing this mission is expressed by a willingness to innovate to advance the gospel.

The first, and perhaps most striking innovation at Antioch, was the establishment of the church itself. In the early years of the Christian movement, the gospel was retained in the Jewish community and the church largely remained in Jerusalem. Exceptions were rare. One early example of Gentile-reaching outreach was Philip's ministry in Samaria (Acts 8:4–13) and later with the Ethiopian eunuch (Acts 8:26–39). Another example was Peter's travels, resulting in his vision of the edible animals preparing him for his visit to Cornelius (Acts 10). These incidents were precursors to the expansion of the gospel in the Gentile world. They stand out as exceptions to the prevailing practice of the early church, which was to witness the gospel primarily to Jews. The persecution of Stephen which prompted the scattering of men like Philip (Acts 8:1–4) and Peter (Acts 9:32–10:48) was also the impetus for other men to travel as far as Antioch (Acts 11:19).

The Bible indicates these anonymous men made their way as far as "Phoenicia, Cyprus, and Antioch, speaking the message to no one except Jews" (Acts 11:19). So far, despite the command of Jesus (Acts 1:8) and the examples of Philip and Peter (the men who traveled to Antioch may or may not have been aware of their work), the early church had remained a Jewish-focused, Jerusalem-contained movement. That was all about to change.

While most itinerant preachers confined their work to Jews, "there were some of them, Cypriot and Cyrenian men, who came to Antioch and began speaking to the Hellenists, proclaiming the good news about the Lord Jesus" (Acts 11:20). These anonymous men—never named in the Bible, identities lost in church history—broke the mold and began preaching the gospel openly in the Gentile community. While that seems like standard operating procedure to Christians today, at the time it was a courageous act by men who risked their lives to innovate the gospel's advance. Generations of Jewish tradition and years of early Christian practice mandated these brave men be circumspect with the gospel. Yet they cast aside all restraint, preached the gospel to the Gentiles, "and a large number who believed turned to the Lord" (Acts 11:21).

These preachers are heroes, giants in Christian history. Unless you are Jewish, you owe a great debt to these men. Without their courageous willingness to innovate—preaching the gospel in a way it had never been preached, to a people who had never heard it, in a city where it had never been shared—you might not be a Christian today. Because of these men, the gospel finally broke the shackles of religious tradition and became good news for all people everywhere.

When you get to heaven, whom do you want to meet? Perhaps Paul, to clarify some of the confusing passages he wrote; Elijah, to hear firsthand the story about fire on the mountain; or Peter and

John, to hear about resurrection morning. For prominent men like this, the line will be long. The fellows who started the church at Antioch probably won't be as busy.

These anonymous heroes, these unknown evangelistic church planters who preached the gospel in Antioch and founded the first church among the Gentiles, deserve eternal accolades. They should be thanked for their courage, for their vision, and for opening the door for Gentiles to become Christians. Knowing Jesus and serving His church make our lives meaningful. These men deserve our gratitude.

A second innovation at Antioch was establishing a teaching ministry, led by Barnabas with Paul's help, to facilitate the continued progress of the gospel among the Gentiles. After Barnabas first arrived in Antioch, he quickly surmised he needed help to ground the new church in sound doctrine and practice. He knew just the man, but bringing him into the mix was radical and controversial. Paul was a former persecutor of the church, who supported the terror-inducing events that sent the preachers to Antioch in the first place. He was also a relatively unproven leader, having spent recent years in relative isolation (Gal. 1:17–24). For these reasons the innovative decision to bring Paul into the church's leadership was both insightful and courageous.

The results of this decision were positive: "For a whole year they [Barnabas and Paul] met with the church and taught large numbers" (Acts 11:26). The evangelistic movement initiated in Antioch stabilized and maintained its momentum under Paul's teaching ministry. Along with Barnabas (Acts 11:24), Paul was responsible for large numbers of people placing faith in Jesus as Savior and learning to live under His lordship.

A third innovation at Antioch was probably not intended by the church but is nonetheless memorable. It was in Antioch that "the disciples were first called Christians" (Acts 11:26). This was most likely a term of derision hung on the early followers of The Way by their critics and detractors. They ridiculed believers as the "Christ ones," men and women who talked so often about "the Christ" they earned a new nickname.

It's not hard to imagine how this moniker may have originated. Early Antioch believers apparently enjoyed talking about "Jesus the Christ" all the time, in every place, with every person. They talked about Christ while shopping in the market, watching athletic events, washing clothes at the river, and working in their shops and fields. They spoke of Christ as the Center of their lives, the One who forgave them, and as the Source of new life. Christ was the focus of their worship and the reason their ethical behavior stood in such sharp contrast to that of unbelievers in their community. Truly they were people enamored with and consumed by Christ and His presence in their lives.

Members of First Church, Antioch apparently had a well-earned reputation for being "Christ talkers." What do the members of your church have a reputation for talking about in the community? Jesus is seldom mentioned by many believers in any secular context. Conversations about Jesus at work, on the ball field, while shopping, or at any other time in everyday life are rare when believers interact with unbelievers. Not in Antioch! Christ dominated their thinking and influenced their interactions to such an extent their vocabulary earned them a nickname that has since become the defining label for the movement initiated by Jesus.

A final significant innovation at Antioch was the initiation of the first intentional missionary movement. During a worship service the Holy Spirit told the church to send Barnabas and Paul on a trip to share the gospel and start new churches in other cities (Acts 13:2). The tone of the story indicates the church responded fairly quickly to those directions and "after they had fasted, prayed, and laid hands on them, they sent them off" (Acts 13:3).

The first trip resulted in new churches started in Cyprus, Pisidian Antioch, Iconium, Lystra, and Derbe. The missionary team eventually returned to Antioch. After they "gathered the church together, they reported everything God had done with them, and that He had opened the door of faith to the Gentiles. And they spent considerable time with the disciples" (Acts 14:27–28). The continued support, interest, and accountability the Antioch church demonstrated for the missionary team is evident in their response to the trip-reporting service. The first journey, however, wasn't the end of the mission endeavors of the church at Antioch.

Eventually Paul and Barnabas separated, ending their partnership in the gospel (Acts 15:36–41) and apparently their personal relationship (as far as is recorded in the Bible). We will analyze their conflict in detail in chapter 7. For now, however, note that when the first missionary team had a significant relational breakdown, the Antioch church maintained its missional focus. When Paul and Barnabas separated, both men chose new partners (Paul chose Silas and Barnabas chose Mark); and both teams, although going separate ways, still took trips to further the mission of the gospel. Clearly, the Gentile church at Antioch had a profound, sustained commitment to spreading the gospel to other cities in the Mediterranean world. Not even a major conflict among its most beloved leaders could derail their commitment to the mission.

The church at Antioch is an example of continued innovation *for spreading the gospel, enlarging the church, and expanding the kingdom.* This church was started by innovative, evangelistic, church planters who had the courage to do something never done before, to preach the gospel broadly among the Gentiles. The church continued under innovative leaders: Barnabas (who had the courage to do what had never been done before, bring Paul on to the teaching team of a church) and Paul (who first ministered prominently in Antioch). They also innovated a new name as an early designation for the movement of Jesus followers. We are called Christians because those Antioch brothers and sisters could not stop talking about Christ. Finally, this amazing church birthed and sustained the fledgling first-century missionary movement. They sent out and supported the first missionaries, setting a pattern for countless churches through the ages who have been inspired to do the same thing. The church at Antioch was an innovative church with an entrepreneurial mind-set riveted on getting the gospel to the whole world.

The innovations at Antioch were all directly related to getting the gospel to more people, in more places, in whatever ways were required to be sure the church grew and the kingdom kept expanding. The church at Antioch was willing to do whatever it took to make sure more and more people were given the opportunity to convert to Jesus. They were relentless in this quest, setting a remarkable example for transformational churches today.

Innovation with a Purpose

Transformational churches innovate. But they innovate for a reason: so more and more people can become Christians. The innovations at Antioch all had a singular focus. Healthy churches today have the same focus and willingness to change, as needed, to continually reach more and more people with the gospel. Transformational churches refuse to settle for less than missional effectiveness and make whatever changes are necessary to ensure the gospel's progress. Innovation for any other reason is counterproductive. Simply copying methods, without developing strategies rooted in an entrepreneurial mind-set focused on kingdom expansion, is superficial and foolish.

When we started a church in Oregon, we adopted a more contemporary worship style including projecting song lyrics with an overhead projector. Wow! I am *old*! As our church grew, other pastors asked for counsel on becoming more seeker friendly and creating churches more oriented toward reaching unbelievers. One pastor both amused and frustrated us. He asked a series of detailed questions about projected lyrics. What songs do you sing? What kind of projector did you buy? Who runs the machine during the service? How do you produce the cells? How are they filed? Blah, blah, blah! He was determined to copy our use of the overhead projector to the minutest detail, believing there was some magic in a machine you could buy in an antique store today.

He missed the point entirely. We were using a worship style that connected with our community and delivery systems that simplified the weekly setup of our portable church. Projecting song lyrics was a methodology, an expression of our mind-set, not a core strategy. Yet he zoned in on this as the key to our effectiveness. He was convinced getting his church to "sing off the screen" would revolutionize their missional effectiveness. Not likely!

Pursuing this kind of change for superfluous reasons frustrates church members and fails to produce lasting positive results. It ignores the proverbial warning: "Sow the wind and reap the whirlwind" (Hos. 8:7). Unfocused change foments a storm of uncertainty and reaps a hurricane of turmoil and conflict. There is a better way. Make sure changes are genuinely and directly connected to reaching more people with the gospel. Most followers will support you when they are convinced the changes you propose will accomplish this purpose. Not all will embrace every change since almost no change is universally supported by everyone. Standing up to opposition when the stakes are legitimate and worth fighting for is different, however, from defending an agenda with a lesser purpose. One is worth the pain. The other is not.

Transformational churches often follow this pattern. They discern what is required to reach people in their community. Then they appraise their situation and strategize for necessary change. Usually, when done well, prayerful submission to the Holy Spirit is evident. Church members (and their leaders) ask for His guidance and power all along the way. While this sounds like a clean process, it's often painful (even divisive) as sacred cows are sacrificed and risks taken by faith. Nonetheless, changes are eventually embraced, and the church moves ahead.

Sometimes, however, an entirely different process happens. Churches spontaneously morph plans into action, surprising themselves with the resulting ministries. Leaders can tell their story in hindsight but have little idea how they achieved their results until after the fact. They discern how God led them, how they intuitively responded, and how change happened naturally. But they do so in hindsight, not with foresight.

Both patterns produce the same result: genuine change affirmed by believers and new people added to the faith. Unfortunately, both patterns also sometimes produce how-to manuals for others to copy for the "guaranteed" results. Avoid this kind of canned approach to church-growth strategies. Learn from as many people as you can, but always analyze your present situation to determine workable strategies and methods for your setting. Be open to the serendipitous, spontaneous changes the Spirit may lead you to adopt, truly new ideas He creates within you and your followers.

The idea of being an innovator may intimidate you. To innovate is to make changes to established patterns or to introduce something new or *as if new*. Being an innovator doesn't necessarily mean you are one of the creative few who thinks of something that has never been done before. It means you are one of the courageous few who are willing to lead others to do what they have never done before. There is a huge difference. There are few Steve Jobs and Bill Gates in the world. But there are thousands of us who can pray, learn, adjust, amend, create, shape, borrow, copy, and occasionally (just kidding!) steal an idea from someone else. Remember, to innovate is to change established patterns, introduce something new or something *as if new*. A five-year-old boy, my youngest son Caleb, taught me this principle.

On the first Sunday after leaving the church we had planted in Oregon to assume a denominational leadership role, we visited a church in another city. It had a more traditional worship style than our church but was nonetheless healthy and growing, reaching people in its community. When the worship leader instructed us to begin the service, she said, "Open your hymnals." I stood and opened a hymnal as instructed. I held the book low so Caleb (an early reader) could sing along.

Caleb tugged on my pants, pointed to the hymnal, and asked, "Daddy, what's this?"

"It's a hymnal, a book with all the songs this church sings in worship," I whispered.

His eyes lit up, "You should get these for our church! Then everyone would have all our songs, and we wouldn't have to set up the projector and screen every Sunday!"

My son, reared in a contemporary church plant, had never *seen* a hymnal. For him it was a stunning innovation, a tool every church should have to facilitate worship. God taught me a fundamental principle about innovation that day: something is innovative, no matter how long it has been around, if it's new to you (or your

followers). So relax. You can innovate, change the established
patterns and introduce new (or as if new) ideas to reach more
people with the gospel. You don't have to create something that has
never been done before. You do have to develop the discernment
to discover God's leadership about what needs to change in your
church. Then you will need courage to make it happen. Change may
not be easy, but it will be worth it as more and more people become
disciples of Jesus.

Institution or Movement?

The Western church, particularly mainline and evangelical
churches in North America, has become more of an institution
than a movement. The early church, including Antioch, was more
a movement than an institution. What's the difference? What
caused the change? Is it possible to reclaim some of the qualities of
a movement in established churches today?

A movement is a spontaneous collaboration of people around a
compelling purpose or agenda. An institution is an organized group
of people who also rally around a core purpose. The difference is
their focus. In a movement the focus is on accomplishing some
greater good outside the needs of the members. Institutions, on
the other hand, often claim an external purpose but create systems
and processes mostly designed to sustain themselves. A movement
usually has limited policies, procedures, and layers of decision-
making. It can seem chaotic unless you are part of the movement.
Then the euphoria of fulfilling a dream overcomes the sense of
being out of control. Institutions thrive on policies, procedure
manuals, and check-and-balance decision-making designed to limit
risk—particularly risk to the institution. Movements are fresh, new,
and often characterized by a sense of urgency based on the need

to succeed in order to survive. Institutions are more stable, with survival no longer an issue, but retaining missional focus an ever-present challenge.

Most local churches began as movements. They were often started by an intrepid church planter with a passion for reaching new people with the gospel. Or perhaps they were started by a core group intentionally sent to a new city or by an existing small group that grew into a church. Occasionally new churches result from church splits. While the conflict can be painful, it's typically felt more intensely and for a longer duration by those left behind than by those who move away. The people who start the new church are moving forward so the conflict recedes more quickly from their awareness. In almost every case, no matter how it begins, a new church has the qualities of a movement. A new church is riveted on reaching new people, focuses more on outsiders than on its own needs, often seems chaotic and (in an appealing way) a little out of control. A new church makes decisions quickly, with little regard for policy (who has time to write them?) or precedent (there isn't any in a new church!). The leaders articulate the mission, the followers embrace it, and decisions flow quickly because everyone answers to one objective: reach people in order to survive as a new church. "Grow or die" can be a powerful motivation.

But as surely as spring turns to summer and summer to fall and then winter, almost all churches eventually evolve from a movement to an institution. As more and more people are added to the membership, organization must be created to manage them and direct their combined efforts. Legal requirements, fiscal management, personnel matters, building construction, and the challenges of managing more and more people (a growing economy of scale) all lead to the development of institutional structures.

This conclusion may surprise you: *institutional development is not entirely a bad outcome!* Developing institutional structures is not, in and of itself, a destructive process for a church. Problems arise, however, when preserving institutional structures at the expense of the mission becomes the priority. How can you keep this from happening? If it has already happened, what can you do to lead your church to be more of a movement and less of an institution?

First, model the movement but manage the institution. As a leader, what you do, what you communicate, and what you magnify by your presence has a profound influence on organizational ethos. As a pastor, magnify aspects of your work contributing to your church's missional focus. For example, devote more time to evangelistic visitation than committee meetings. When you communicate about your work (in sermons, blogs, or hallway conversations), talk more about your missional activities than church management issues. For me that means talking with students about sharing the gospel with friends and leading Bible studies for young men rather than telling them about meetings with auditors or attorneys. Manage your organization quietly. Magnify your mission and your investment in accomplishing it by communicating more about the missional aspects of your work than the institutional components.

Second, help followers remember when your church was a movement. Learn your church's founding story and tell it from time to time. Use anniversaries and other historical celebrations to commemorate the "movement days" when your founders took great risks to start your church. Remind your members of the spirit of sacrifice and adventure that created your church. It's easy for church members with a short memory to be confused about the causes of church health. One church grew from a few dozen people to an attendance near one thousand over a thirty-year period. When the long-time pastor retired, the church sought a pastor who could sustain the church's strength. Three pastors and ten years later, the church is still in decline. They continue to search for a pastor who will restore them to "doing what we have always done and done well." They have missed the point of what made them a strong church in the first place. They have not "always done" anything. They started with a spirit of innovation, a willingness to adjust and change to facilitate effectiveness, and maintained that spirit for years. The secret to their success was continual change led by a pastor focused on advancing the gospel. When he left, the focus shifted to institutionalizing his methods rather than continuing his strategy. Trying to preserve what they had, the church has become resistant to change and determined to stay "with what has always worked." Unfortunately, what always worked wasn't their programs and ministry style they still cherish. They have lost the spirit of innovation and change.

Third, celebrate missional progress more than institutional success. Related to this, when possible, link every institutional achievement to the mission of advancing the gospel. For example, connect building programs to creating space for unbelievers to learn about Jesus. Connect adding staff to enlarging the capacity for equipping people to be on mission. Connect fund-raising to accomplishing projects that change lives. Connect creating committee structures and organizational policies to simplifying decision-making so everyone can invest more time in missional activities. Magnify and celebrate missional success stories over institutional progress. Do this with integrity. People can spot a phony appeal for their money or time. When a change can't be legitimately linked to the church's mission, avoid making the change or make it quietly and move on rather than linking it dubiously or tangentially to the mission.

One denominational leader devoted his annual report to progress on bylaw revisions and budget reformatting. Those things may have needed to be done and reported in three minutes rather than thirty. The bulk of the report should have been devoted to the missional activity of the churches he coordinated and their shared impact advancing the gospel through common projects. Followers watch what leaders celebrate and commemorate and then invest themselves in similar activities. Make sure you celebrate being a movement more than preserving an institution. Doing so will facilitate the entrepreneurial spirit necessary for embracing change in a transformational church.

Questions for Reflection

1. What has been your worst change experience? What went wrong? What did you learn about leading change through this experience?

2. Why do you initiate change? Are you focused on the mission of advancing the gospel or do you have other agendas prompting changes you suggest?

3. What are the four major innovations from the Antioch church discussed in this chapter? Which one would require the most change to emulate in your church?

4. Are you an innovator? Are you willing to try new things, or "as if new" things, in order to advance the gospel? What innovations does your church need to adopt to fulfill its mission more effectively? On a scale of 1 to 10, how open is your church to innovation and change? What will you do to move the needle on the meter?

◄●►

5. Is your church more of an institution or a movement? What qualities of each are most helpful to your church right now? Most limiting? On a continuum of 1 to 10, with "movement" on one end and "institution" on the other end, where would you place your church? Which way does it need to move? What will you do to lead this change?

Chapter 5

A Disciple-Making Community

A transformational church changes lives.

Following Jesus in community is one of the primary ways Christians are shaped to become more like Jesus. At least that's the way church is supposed to work. God designed the church to be a transformational community. It welcomes sinners, assimilates new believers as members, and shapes them into fully devoted Jesus followers. The Lord explained this when He spoke what is commonly called the Great Commission, "All authority has been given to Me in heaven and on earth. Go, therefore, and make disciples of all nations, baptizing them in the name of the Father and of the Son and of the Holy Spirit, teaching them to observe everything I have commanded you. And remember, I am with you always, to the end of the age" (Matt. 28:18–20).

Because English translations often put "go" at the beginning of verse 19, usually capitalized and set apart with a comma, readers incorrectly assume the emphasis in this passage is on going. This interpretation is strengthened by our evangelical propensity for missions and evangelism. We know we should be going, so we emphasize this aspect of Jesus' instructions. But the linguistic emphasis in this passage is on making disciples, not going. To capture the appropriate emphasis, consider this slight adjustment to the above translation: "Go, therefore, and *make disciples.*" Understanding the Great Commission with those words emphasized will help us keep the emphasis straight. Jesus told His followers to make disciples by baptizing and teaching, both activities that can only be done in community. (Think about it—at least two people are required for either activity!)

While baptism signifies entry into a new lifestyle, the primary means the church uses to develop disciples is teaching. Teaching shapes the mind. As new thoughts emerge, new attitudes and actions result. Paul amplified these ideas when he wrote, "The weapons of our warfare are not fleshly, but are powerful through God for the demolition of strongholds. We demolish arguments and every high-minded thing that is raised up against the knowledge of God, taking every thought captive to the obedience of Christ" (2 Cor. 10:4–5). Spiritual growth is rooted in changed thinking. Carnal thought patterns, the strongholds of "arguments and every high-minded thing that is raised up against the knowledge of God," naturally dominate the minds of unbelievers and new believers. Learning God's Word and God's ways takes time and may call for undoing years of wrong thinking and learning to think biblically and to behave accordingly. The best word to describe this process is *transformation.*

The theological word for this is *sanctification.* While that word literally means "to make holy," the doctrine of sanctification broadly encompasses all aspects of spiritual transformation. While *justification* describes your once-in-a-moment conversion experience, *sanctification* involves a lifetime of spiritual growth, change, and development. Sanctification is becoming more like Jesus, God's process of every believer's being "conformed to the image of His Son" (Rom. 8:29). While this process is personal, it wasn't designed to be accomplished in isolation. Spiritual formation requires a group effort.

The biblical metaphors for churches are collective descriptors implying life, growth, and change. The church, for example, is called the body of Christ (1 Cor. 12:12–31), a temple of living stones (1 Pet. 2:5), branches on a vine (John 15:5), and the family of God (1 Pet. 4:17). All of these images communicate the corporate nature of church life and spiritual growth. Through their teaching ministry, churches play a vital role in personal discipleship. A church provides biblical instruction necessary for spiritual formation. Paul admonishes believers to "not be conformed to this age, but be transformed by the renewing of your mind, so that you may discern what is the good, pleasing, and perfect will of God" (Rom. 12:2). The mind is renewed through new information, biblical truth, producing the enlightenment necessary for God-honoring choices. Through this process a believer develops "the mind of Christ" (1 Cor. 2:16) or the capacity to consider, reason, and understand life from a biblical perspective or worldview.

This type of transformation—a renewed mind producing new choices based on an ingrained biblical worldview—should be a church's goal for every member. Disciple-making in a corporate context leads to personal renewal. Spiritual formation, spiritual growth, and spiritual maturity all describe becoming more and more like Jesus in character and actions. While the results are personal, the best context for producing these changes is the fellowship of a church. While the results are individual, the ultimate conclusion is corporate—a transformed and transformational church.

How Are We Doing?

Since disciple-making is the mandate and transformation the desired outcome, the logical question is, how are we doing? How is the church, particularly the church in North America, doing in fulfilling the Lord's instructions to make disciples? How transformed is the typical believer or church? Is there evidence of a renewed mind leading to new choices producing lifestyle changes among most Christians? Are churches today communities of individuals undergoing renovation? Is personal renewal a normal result of church activities and ministries?

In his book *The Shape of Faith to Come*, Brad Waggoner reports the implications of a comprehensive study of twenty-five hundred American church members. Waggoner's study reveals alarming realities. His findings show profound inadequacies in current approaches by American evangelical churches. On a simple scale to measure spiritual formation (including knowledge of basic doctrinal and behavioral qualities expected of Christians), the study showed only 17 percent of American believers had an acceptable score of at least 80 percent.[12] When the categories were narrowed to twelve core Christian beliefs, less than 60 percent of churchgoers gave acceptable answers approximating theological orthodoxy.[13] After a year the sample group was again surveyed to determine the level of spiritual growth that had occurred. Waggoner concluded, after a full year, "There was little evidence of overall spiritual development in our sample of churchgoers."[14] In short, churches are simply not teaching for transformation, developing doctrinal insight and behavioral changes among believers.

It's tempting to dismiss these results as too limited ("after all, it's only one study") or somehow flawed ("they didn't study my church"). But the study isn't too limited or somehow flawed.

It's brutally honest and corroborated by similar studies by Gallup, Barna, Pew Research, LifeWay Research,[15] and other organizations tracking American church life. The beliefs and behaviors of American Christians aren't much different than their secular counterparts. In biblical language the church looks a lot like the world. Transformation, on an appropriate scale, just isn't happening through many (if not most) churches today. Transformational churches producing maturing disciples are the exception. Emulating churches who are effectively teaching for transformation must be our goal. Once again let's turn to our ancient model in Antioch for help with a contemporary problem.

The Teaching Ministry at Antioch

The church at Antioch started almost entirely though conversion growth when itinerant preachers first shared the gospel with Gentiles. As the church formed, the only experienced believers were the church planters, later adding Barnabas and Paul as pastoral leaders. Probably few new believers in Antioch had much biblical background or worldview. While there was a Jewish community in Antioch, the early believers were Gentiles who most likely had little knowledge of the Old Testament. The church started with converts who had limited biblical knowledge and a secular worldview. If they did have a spiritual perspective prior to conversion (likely, given the religious pluralism of the city), it certainly wasn't a Christian outlook.

This is still the pattern today for church planting in many places, even in the United States. When we started a church in Oregon, most of our early converts had limited biblical knowledge. One friend, Steve, started our conversation about the Bible by asking, "What's a testament?" Another new believer, coincidentally also named Steve, accompanied me to speak in a conference at a local church. He stood in the back of the auditorium, gazed around the room, then turned to me and said, "So this is what a church looks like." Since our church met in a public school, he had never been inside a "real" church building. Both of these men were in their mid-thirties, professionals with families. One had never opened a Bible, and the other had never been inside a church building. These men became believers and later leaders in our new church. The early converts at Antioch were like these men—secular, recently saved, in need of transformation into maturing disciples.

Soon after the church at Antioch began, Barnabas arrived from Jerusalem. He surveyed the situation, "encouraged all of them to remain true to the Lord," and observed "large numbers of people were added to the Lord" (Acts 11:23–24). Barnabas realized two things: he needed a strategy to solidify the church, and he needed help to accomplish it. To solve the problem, he took an unusual step: he left town for a few days! Barnabas "went to Tarsus [about eighty-five miles away] to search for Saul [Paul], and when he found him he brought him to Antioch" (Acts 11:25–26). Paul was the leader he needed. Now Barnabas could implement his strategy for turning new converts into a functioning church.

The two-pronged strategy Barnabas and Paul implemented is summarized in these simple words: "For a whole year they met with the church and taught large numbers" (Acts 11:26). The most obvious part of the strategy is the teaching ministry they launched. But the second aspect is the intentionality and continuity of their work. They taught the church "for a whole year"—regularly, systematically, thoroughly, repetitively, then all over again and again. The continual stream of new believers coming into the church would have required this approach to keep everyone moving toward maturity in Christ.

What did they teach? No curriculum is described in Acts but one result of their teaching—"the disciples were first called Christians in Antioch" (Acts 19:26)—strongly implies the subject matter. The subject was Jesus Christ—informed by Paul's extensive knowledge of the Old Testament, his personal encounter with Jesus, his early instruction by other Christian leaders, and his developing theological convictions and practical conclusions (soon to be expressed as letters to other churches in the form of New Testament epistles).

Beyond Barnabas's and Paul's teaching ministries, Acts includes other examples of teaching and the value placed on spiritual instruction at Antioch. During the early years the church hosted guest preachers. Agabus, from Jerusalem, "stood up and predicted by the Spirit that there would be a severe famine throughout the Roman world" (Acts 11:28). Later, when the outcome of the Jerusalem Council was reported in Antioch, Judas and Silas were invited to preach. They "encouraged the brothers and strengthened them with a long message" (Acts 15:32, a favorite verse for preachers everywhere—*a long message!*). After that, Paul and Barnabas resumed their ministry in Antioch "teaching and proclaiming the message of the Lord" (Acts 15:35). Besides these brothers, the other leaders at Antioch—including Simeon, Lucius, and Manaen—were also known as "prophets and teachers" (Acts 13:1).

Another situation, its response to false teachers, also underscores the importance the Antioch church placed on its teaching ministry. Some men from Judea arrived in Antioch and taught, "Unless you are circumcised according to the custom prescribed by Moses, you cannot be saved!" (Acts 15:1). This was the original controversy that had prompted Barnabas's first visit to Antioch rearing its ugly head again. The Antioch Christians had long since settled this issue, but nonetheless Paul and Barnabas had to engage in public debate with these visiting teachers. The church at Antioch eventually arranged for a traveling party to go to Jerusalem to settle the controversy once for all (Acts 15:2). The group was "sent on their way by the church" (Acts 15:3) with confidence the issue could be and would be settled in the Jerusalem church. (Thus ending this doctrinal debate forever, or so they hoped.)

While this is an example of the church at Antioch rejecting false teachers, it still indicates the high regard they had for instruction in the early church. It also leads us to consider the outcome of teaching in Antioch. Did teaching in Antioch produce transformation? Did life change result? Did the disciple-making efforts of Paul, Barnabas, and other teachers and guest preachers facilitate changed attitudes and behaviors? There is clear evidence in Acts in the affirmative. At least five examples of transformation emerge from the story of Antioch. These same areas are still paramount for believers today.

Transforming Lives in Antioch

Teaching the gospel, along with its implications and applications, changed lives in Antioch. From the fallow ground of Gentile secularism, a vibrant church emerged in a relatively short time. Men and women who had no Christian background and little prior exposure to a biblical worldview were soon demonstrating the wisdom and character of Jesus in decisions and actions.

The church at Antioch was transformed in its understanding of the gospel and the importance of preserving its purity. When false teachers tried to convince them that something other than God's grace through faith was required for salvation, they confronted the heretics and encouraged their leaders to seek a public and potentially controversial resolution (Acts 15:1–2). The next chapter will consider doctrinal integrity in greater detail as a mark of a transformational church. For now, simply note the transformation that occurred in Antioch. From knowing nothing about the gospel and little about the Scriptures to standing up for the gospel and demanding its defense by their leaders, the people of Antioch morphed into a church with sound doctrinal convictions.

The Antioch believers were also transformed in their understanding of financial resources and using money to further kingdom work. Early Christians and churches were often poor. There's no reason to believe Antioch was any different. Yet, when offered the opportunity to give to famine relief (Acts 11:28–30), they did so willingly and generously. They gave "each . . . according to his ability" (Acts 11:29), indicating personal transformation had occurred. More than a corporate gift given from previously pooled funds, this was an offering given by individuals. Each person gave, in proportion to their ability, with a sense of shared sacrifice being a worthy goal. Being taught Christian stewardship probably established the foundation for this offering.

A third evidence of transformation is the church's value of and participation in corporate worship services. Previously, these Gentiles may have participated in all manner of cultic worship practices involving everything from animal sacrifice to sexual debauchery. Through its teaching ministry (and modeling by its leaders), the Antioch church developed worship practices that included hearing and responding to preaching, giving offerings, prayer, fasting, discerning the Holy Spirit's leading, and commissioning missionaries through laying on hands (Acts 11:27–30; 13:2–3). These may have been similar to some of their former pagan practices, but learning to do them in the Spirit reflected the distinctive Christian aspects of their worship services.

Another example of transformation was sending missionaries and sustaining them through multiple mission trips. The people in Antioch progressed from being an object of missionary outreach to a church sending missionaries while still first-generation believers. That's rapid progress! Related to this is the personal transformation of individuals into witnesses. This resulted in the title "Christian" first being used in Antioch. As previously mentioned, this was probably a term used by outsiders to describe the early believers. Their personal transformation, and resulting public witness, was so profound it earned them a derisive nickname they wore with pride. The corporate expression of this change later resulted in the church's launching the first missionary movement.

Finally, the church at Antioch developed significant problem-solving skills rooted in their understanding of church membership and fellowship. Accountability for doctrinal and missional decisions was a normal part of church life in Antioch. They successfully solved the conflict about the gospel by graciously receiving the decision of the Jerusalem church (Acts 15:30–35). They also successfully resolved the conflict between Barnabas and Paul over John Mark by creating two missionary teams and preserving the church's support for missions (Acts 15:36–41).

By any measure the church at Antioch is a model of transformation. Through its teaching ministry, in obedience to Jesus' instructions, disciples were made in Antioch. Doctrinal convictions were established, stewardship was learned and practiced, worship was cultivated, witnessing and missionary outreach flourished, and church problems were solved by applying principles of the gospel in interpersonal relationships. The spring from which these changes emerged was new birth in Jesus. The channel which guided the flow toward maturity was the teaching ministries of Paul, Barnabas, Agabus, Judas, Silas, Simeon, Lucius, and Manaen (and possibly others). Antioch is an inspiring model of a teaching church. It's a good example of a church making disciples, men and women renewing their minds and learning to act more and more like Jesus.

Teaching for Transformation Today

Most churches have some type of teaching program offering services, classes, courses, and/or seminars on a variety of subjects. Simply having a teaching program however, based on evidence already cited, apparently isn't enough to produce life transformation. Healthy churches teach strategically, with measureable steps of progress guiding people toward specific outcomes through their instructional ministry. Transformational churches hold people accountable for spiritual growth, particularly regarding membership standards and leadership qualifications. Those standards and qualifications include both informational and behavioral components. Disciple-making churches have a template, imperfect as it may be, of what a "discipled Christian" looks like. These churches steadily move people toward those qualities and capabilities. These churches take a strategic approach to their teaching ministry in both content and methodology. Here are some key aspects of each of these as expressed in transformational churches today.

Strategic Qualities of a Teaching Ministry

When considering the Antioch model, as well as observing effective disciple-making churches today, three strategic qualities of an effective teaching ministry emerge. The first is *intentionality*. At Antioch, Barnabas saw the significant need for a teaching ministry and promptly left town. That may seem like a callous response. He soon returned with Paul. Barnabas's departure wasn't shirking responsibility or avoiding the problem. It was a strategic retreat. He had a plan but knew he needed the right leader to launch the effort. Barnabas made an intentional choice to take his time, get the right leader, and launch a sustainable effort.

Transformational churches do more than just schedule a random set of classes or seminars. They create a planned program designed to move people from conversion (or in some cases preconversion) to maturity in their faith. Some methods frequently used to create this type of plan will be described later in this chapter.

The Antioch model also reveals a *comprehensive* approach to shaping lives. As already outlined, the believers in Antioch were changed in many ways. They learned Christian doctrine, financial stewardship, worship practices, witnessing methods, missionary methods, conflict management, and principles of maintaining church fellowship. This list isn't meant to encompass everything taught in Antioch or what should be taught by a healthy church today, but it would be a good starting point!

Transformational churches have a comprehensive program of training people in all aspects of the Christian life from doctrine to stewardship to witnessing to missionary involvement to ministry skill development. This might sound like a daunting task for any church except the largest churches, but it is possible to do these things in a small church, including a church plant. A comprehensive approach doesn't mean all these subjects are taught simultaneously. It means the church has an intentional plan to move its members through a process of developing in these areas. This takes time, which leads to the next aspect of a strategic plan for making disciples.

The third quality of a strategic approach to a teaching ministry is *repetition*. In Antioch, Paul's initial teaching ministry lasted a full year. It was more than one sermon or seminar. It was a continuing, repetitive, progressive effort. All through the year, new people were becoming believers, while at the same time other believers were advancing at different rates in their spiritual development. The reality of continued conversions and varying levels of spiritual maturity mandated continually starting from the beginning with new believers while helping more mature Christians keep growing—all at the same time. Disciple-making in a growing church is demanding.

Transformational churches establish foundational studies and repeat them over and over again, sometimes for years. One church established a new member class to teach the church's mission, vision, values, and core strategies to every new member. They maintained the same approach to training new members for more than *ten years*! As the years rolled past, the momentum of hundreds of people thoroughly versed in the same mission, vision, values, and core strategies had a compounding effect. The church was resolutely committed to its core purposes and enjoyed remarkable unity in the midst of continued, sometimes rapid growth and change.

Another church determined ten key issues or practices (ranging from "security of the believer" to "how to give your testimony") they wanted every new believer to master. For adults and teenagers they established a one-on-one discipleship program, with each pair working together for three to four months to complete these basic studies. A different strategy was used with children. As newer members completed the studies, they were recruited to take even newer converts or members through the program, further reinforcing their initial study as they worked through the material a second time with their trainee. The church continued this process for years, building a cadre of people who were established in their faith and equipped with the essentials for living the Christian life.

A third church identified a set of subjects it felt should be consistently repeated in its discipleship program. They determined subjects like Christian doctrine, money management, marriage, parenting, witnessing, and ministry skill development (like teacher training, deacon service, etc.) should be taught over and over again. For years this church hosted an ongoing semester-style program of courses related to these subjects. Sometimes the same course was repeated year after year. In other cases, like on marriage, a different perspective was taken each time the subject came around in the rotation. The key was repetition of the same subjects year after year. While only a small percentage (compared to the Sunday worship attendance) of the church was involved in these courses at any given time, over time a large percentage of the church's members participated. People respond based on their needs. The church set out a continual buffet of spiritual growth opportunities. Members ate what they needed, when they needed it, and grew accordingly.

All these churches arbitrarily determined the content of their respective programs. The power of their approach was repetition, not necessarily the content of the material. No church has the final answer on exactly what every believer in every context needs to know to be established as a new convert or functional as a new member. But every church can determine, in its setting, the essentials it deems necessary. After some trial and error to finalize the process, a long-term commitment will lead to prolonged effectiveness and a compounding effect of collective spiritual formation. One of the key challenges for all churches is replicating this process for all age groups, but that is also one of the most enjoyable aspects of multigenerational ministry through the church.

Strategic Methods of a Teaching Program

While the strategy and outcomes for a teaching ministry can be discovered in Antioch, the record of the specific teaching methods they used isn't as clear. Methodology isn't much of an emphasis in Acts or in the Bible in general. Methods are strongly influenced by cultural factors like ethnicity, geography, gender, and age. Methods also change rapidly, going in and out of style generation by generation. For these reasons the Bible focuses more on principles than methods. We do well to follow that pattern and maintain methodological flexibility. Here, then, are five approaches commonly used by disciple-making churches today. Within each approach there's wide latitude for developing specific methods to accomplish discipleship goals in each unique ministry setting.

First, one-on-one pairs are same-gender partners who commit to work together toward a specific training goal. These pairs usually last a few months and work through a prescribed curriculum. They are often used to solidify new believers in their faith or teach a specific skill set to a maturing believer. The leader is usually a more mature Christian (in the case of helping a new believer) or a veteran leader (in the case of shaping a specific skill set). One-on-one pairs work best when there is a definite time frame for training, a prescribed curriculum to master, and an expectation the trainee will eventually help another person through the same process. This approach can be problematic when it devolves into lay counseling or when one of the partners becomes codependent on the other.

My formative years as a believer and early training as a Christian leader were positively shaped by these types of relationships. Various men worked to solidify my faith as a young believer and later to develop specific ministry skills. That church also facilitated these pairings for college students to disciple high school and middle school students one semester at a time. Beginning with participation in that program as a college student and continuing through multiple relationships with men while in pastoral ministry, one-on-one training has been an important disciple-making approach throughout my ministry.

Second, "closed" small groups meet for a limited duration with a finite membership. They form for a purpose, to work through a specific study or meet a specific need. Once they form, the bonding required and the vulnerability expected limits the participation to those who have committed to the group. These groups work well when they meet for a specific time frame (like a few months or a semester) and process toward specific outcomes. They can be troublesome when they become cliquish, continuing indefinitely as a self-appointed group of spiritual elitists.

Third, "open" small groups meet regularly, in a continuing format, and welcome guests or new members at every opportunity. Most Sunday school classes and many home groups function like this. Their studies are open-ended, inviting participation on a week-by-week basis (in contrast to the closed group that requires continuity). Their membership is also more fluid, often with a stated goal of reproducing the class or group. These groups work well when they maintain their identity and focus, resisting the temptation to become de facto closed groups. They also work well for assimilating new people and helping them begin the process of spiritual growth in a less threatening environment than a closed small group or a one-on-one pair.

Fourth, seminars or conferences take many forms ranging from one-day workshops to weekend retreats to classes offered over a few weeks or months. These lend themselves to general presentations with limited accountability. They can be helpful on subjects like marriage or finances where a person may need help but may not be ready to divulge their struggles in a small group or one-on-one relationship. They can also be helpful to introduce content-oriented subjects like doctrinal studies or ministry skill development. The primary weakness for this approach is diminished accountability and limited coaching toward specific applications.

Fifth, preaching, declaring truth from Scripture, is an important teaching tool. While preaching isn't the only teaching approach used in strong churches, pastors of healthy churches use the pulpit as a pedagogical platform. Preaching has content, the gospel and its applications and implications. The strength of this tool is its ability to confront, sobering an audience with the power of the declared Word of God and the standard of living it demands. The only weakness of preaching as a teaching method is depending on it exclusively, without using the other approaches outlined above to build an intentional, comprehensive, repeatable disciple-making strategy. Preaching should buttress the total strategy, not displace it.

Transformational churches use all of these approaches in some combination to make disciples. There is no one-size-fits-all approach that assures spiritual formation. Some subjects, for example, are best taught in small groups. Others are better taught one-on-one. Some people respond better in closed groups while others find them too threatening. A large group approach works better for some believers until they develop the security to risk greater vulnerability in a small group or one-on-one relationship.

A Community of Change

Transformational churches use a "layered" approach rather than a sequential approach to making disciples. A layered approach means the church uses multiple methods at the same time to train disciples. This means some members will be in one-on-one relationships, others in closed groups, others in open groups, while still others only in large groups. Some will participate in multiple opportunities at various levels at the same time. Others will participate in more than one level but on a pick-and-choose basis. Rather than a "you all come" approach that seeks to involve every member in every learning activity, a healthy church creates a menu and challenges people to engage the process at the appropriate level. Leaders aren't passive in this process. Like children who need to eat their vegetables, believers need to be challenged and coached to participate in some learning events they "need" more than they "want." Leaders shepherd people toward the good grass in green pastures even though some sheep may not know they need those elements in their diet.

Transformational churches also use a "coaching" approach to making disciples. Both younger converts and maturing members are encouraged to learn by doing—like sharing the gospel, going on a mission trip, making a hospital visit, providing lay counseling, or teaching a class—with a mentor coaching their performance. This approach should be woven through the teaching program and methods described above, allowing a trainee on-the-job learning. Too much classroom time equates Christian growth with intellectual assent. A solid disciple-making strategy involves coaching people through the growing pains of implementing what they are learning. Becoming a disciple is partly about learning new information, but it is also about transforming behavior, changing the way life is lived. A coaching component to a church's teaching ministry contributes to this process.

A transformational church is a context for change, a community of change. In a transformational church, people are continually learning new insights about themselves, the Christian life, their ever-evolving life circumstances, and how to apply the gospel to their situation. A church should be a safe place to confess sins, admit shortcomings, and find the mutual support necessary to develop a Christian lifestyle. Through its teaching ministry, a church continually instructs, corrects, reproves, and rebukes its members, as well as gives them practical instruction and interpersonal support to apply what they are learning. It's a continuing process. It requires implementation of an intentional, comprehensive, repetitive plan. Layering and coaching buttress the various methods selected and shaped by the local context. Healthy churches settle for nothing less than spiritual growth through personal and corporate transformation. Transformational churches change lives.

Questions for Reflection

1. What has contributed the most to your spiritual growth? How has the church's teaching ministry shaped you? Who have been your best teachers? Why?

2. What key subjects should be taught in a church discipleship program? What are the key issues for new believers? What are the common subjects all believers need to consider over and over again?

3. Does your church have an identified disciple-making process? Is its disciple-making process intentional, comprehensive, and repetitive? If not, how can you improve it?

※◈※

4. Does your church use all five teaching approaches listed in this chapter? Which are most effective? Which need to be included to improve your strategy?

※◈※

5. Do you observe transformation taking place in church members? As a sample, choose ten members and ask, "How have you grown spiritually in the past year?" Rate your church's overall disciple-making process on a scale of 1 to 10. What can you do to move your church toward greater effectiveness as a life-changing community?

Chapter 6

Doctrinal Convictions

A transformational church maintains
doctrinal integrity.

❈ *Doctrine* can be a polarizing word. It sounds dry and boring to some, divisive and legalistic to others. Churches sometimes soften their doctrinal positions, or at least mute their intensity, to lessen this tension and become more attractive to unbelievers. That effort, though well intended, is a misapplication of Paul's example of becoming "all things to all people, so that I may by all means save some" (1 Cor. 9:22). Flexibility in missionary lifestyle doesn't equal and must not include compromising doctrinal integrity, especially truth about the gospel. In Antioch, Paul broke new ground in contextualizing the gospel's presentation but without compromising its message. On the contrary, he undertook extreme measures to defend its purity. Jesus taught a clear gospel. Paul and other New Testament writers articulated its theological nuances as well as its implications for daily living. Healthy churches uphold the gospel and its discipleship demands for believers. Transformational churches stand for truth rather than dilute the message and explain away its requirements for holy living.

Not only is a dilution strategy biblically irresponsible; it's also practically ineffective. Churches with strong doctrinal convictions grow faster and attract the unchurched in greater numbers than compromising churches. Unbelievers, including those with little or no church background, intuitively know a church is supposed to stand for something. When starting a church in Oregon, we considered dropping the denominational label from our name. We postulated it might be a barrier for some who were prejudiced against our particular brand of Christianity. What we discovered was the opposite. As we met unbelievers and told them we were starting a church, their inevitable question was, "What kind of church?" Initially, we gave a general answer like, "A church for the community," or, "A church that follows Jesus." The unchurched then usually asked, "But what *kind of church*—Methodist, Lutheran, Mormon?" When we told them, "Baptist," their response was usually positive, sometimes followed by the question, "Why didn't you just say that in the first place?" It often seemed we were more put off by the label than the people we were trying to reach. And worse, it seemed to them we were duplicitous in our answer, raising questions about our credibility.

This chapter isn't about advocating for or against using a denominational label in your church's name. There are denominationally labeled churches without doctrinal convictions and generically named churches standing strong on biblical principles. My story only contrasts our reluctance to take a doctrinal position for fear of offending outsiders with their expectation a church will naturally advocate biblical convictions. Most unchurched people expect churches to stand for certain beliefs and practices. If we claim to be Christian believers, their expectation is we believe in Someone (Jesus) and in something

(His teachings, expanded to include the entire New Testament). Anything less seems out of character for genuine Christians.

A transformational church holds doctrinal convictions without malice or rancor but with confidence and certainty. Their leaders aren't afraid to declare truth as revealed in Scripture and call people to submit to its authority. What is unappealing to unbelievers (and most Christians) is a church declaring its dogma with anger, legalistic overtones, or a judgmental spirit. Unfortunately, some believers (and their leaders) equate maintaining doctrinal integrity with mean-spirited, aggressive, arrogant behavior. Sound doctrine can be, and should be, declared and defended while still showing the fruit of the Spirit. Holding doctrinal convictions, intensely yet without compromise, is possible, while practicing the humility produced by quiet confidence in the truth of Scripture. The Antioch church and its leaders modeled this balance. We must learn to do the same.

To Cut or Not to Cut, That Was the Question

The first great doctrinal challenge faced by the church at Antioch (and the first-century church in general) was the nature of the gospel. The problem was rooted in a wrong assumption by Jewish Christians that the gospel had to remain connected to their community. Early Jewish believers welcomed converts from non-Jewish backgrounds but felt coming to faith in Jesus also involved becoming Jewish. These Christians have been called Judaizers because of their emphasis on combining the Christian faith with Jewish practice. The defining issue for them was circumcision, requiring a man to undergo this outward act (along with placing faith in Jesus for salvation) as part of identifying with the still largely Jewish Christian community.

Circumcision was the mark of the covenant God established through Abraham with the Jewish people. When God called Abraham, He said, "I am God Almighty. Live in My presence and be devout. I will establish My covenant between Me and you, and I will multiply you greatly. . . . This is My covenant, which you are to keep, between Me and you and your offspring after you: Every one of your males must be circumcised. You must circumcise the flesh of your foreskin to serve as a sign of the covenant between Me and you" (Gen. 17:1, 10–11). For many centuries Jews had practiced circumcision as a symbolic reminder of their unique covenant relationship with God. Giving up this practice was unthinkable since it would compromise the covenant. Inviting others into a covenant relationship with God and signifying their commitment through circumcision would preserve Jewish identity and obedience to God. Since Christianity originated in the Jewish community and the first Christians were Jews, their natural assumption was the path to becoming a Christian and entering a covenant relationship with God included circumcision. That erroneous assumption set the stage for the first significant doctrinal showdown in the church.

After several years of growth among Jews, the Holy Spirit pressed the gospel into new frontiers. As we have already learned, the earliest and most dramatic expansion of the gospel among Gentiles occurred when itinerant preachers "came to Antioch and began speaking to the Hellenists, proclaiming the good news about the Lord Jesus" (Acts 11:20). For the first time the gospel spread rapidly among non-Jews. People were becoming believers and entering a new kind of covenant relationship with God. Tensions soon arose, however, over the issue of circumcision and its implication, the true nature of being the covenant people of God.

To address those tensions, Barnabas was dispatched from the Jewish church in Jerusalem to investigate the situation in Gentile Antioch (Acts 11:22–23). When he arrived, Barnabas affirmed what was happening and brought in Paul to begin the teaching ministry previously described in chapter 5. Barnabas was sent as an investigator but quickly assumed a pastoral role. The expectation of the Jerusalem church was that Barnabas would stop the practice of Gentiles becoming Christians without including covenant-making circumcision as part of their commitment ritual. Barnabas surprised them all by doing just the opposite—facilitating the Gentile-centric, circumcision-less gospel movement in Antioch and helping it grow by leaps and bounds (Acts 11:24). The stage was now set for a major conflict between the two groups over the nature of the gospel.

The Fight over the Gospel

After a while, possibly frustrated by Barnabas's response and action (or inaction, depending on the perspective), "some men came down from Judea [to Antioch] and began to teach the brothers: 'Unless you are circumcised according to the custom prescribed by Moses, you cannot be saved!'" (Acts 15:1). Luke, the author of Acts, hints at his perspective on the debate about to unfold in his choice of two words, *men* and *brothers*. "Men" came down from Judea and spoke to the "brothers" about their supposedly aberrant views regarding the gospel. Even in the introduction to his description of the conflict, Luke affirms the authenticity of the Gentile converts by calling them "brothers."

When the Judean preachers arrived, their message wasn't well received by Paul and Barnabas who "engaged them in serious argument and debate" (Acts 15:2). What do those words mean?

What was the scene like? It's hard to imagine a docile event conducted by the rules of modern debate. Paul and Barnabas were skilled speakers, experienced teachers, and much-loved pastors defending their Gentile flock. "Serious argument and debate" indicates an intense public confrontation as rival teachers declared differing convictions about the gospel.

A barometer of the intensity of this confrontation is Paul's description of these events in Galatians 2.[16] He wrote of the men who advocated circumcision, "This issue arose because of false brothers smuggled in, who came in secretly to spy on our freedom that we have in Christ Jesus, in order to enslave us. But we did not yield in submission to these people for even an hour, so that the truth of the gospel would remain for you" (Gal. 2:4–5). Paul questioned the spiritual status ("false brothers") and ultimate purpose ("to spy on our freedom . . . in order to enslave us") of the circumcision group. Furthermore, the passion of his opposition to this perversion of the gospel is revealed in his claim, "We did not yield in submission to these people for even an hour." When Paul heard circumcision claimed as essential for salvation, he immediately confronted this false doctrine. He was on his feet, possibly even interrupting the speakers, not tolerating false teaching in the Antioch church for even "one hour." Lest you still doubt Paul's intensity, consider his sarcastic broadside leveled at those who taught that a small cut was essential to salvation. He wrote, "I wish that those who are disturbing you might also get themselves castrated!" (Gal. 5:12). Ouch! Paul seems to be saying, "If a little cut is helpful, why not go all the way?"

After this confrontation (or perhaps multiple confrontations over several days), the Antioch church "arranged for Paul and Barnabas and some others of them to go up to the apostles and elders in Jerusalem concerning this controversy" (Acts 15:2). Clearly the problem wasn't worked out to the satisfaction of the Judean preachers because Paul and Barnabas would not relent in their convictions about the gospel. Luke's travelogue again reveals his perspective on the problem and foreshadows the ultimate outcome. As Paul and Barnabas traveled to Jerusalem, "they passed through both Phoenicia and Samaria, explaining in detail the conversion of the Gentiles, and they created great joy among all the brothers" (Acts 15:3). Luke celebrated the gospel, as preached by Paul and Barnabas, and recorded its continued progress while on the way to the meeting supposedly to determine its veracity.

When the traveling party reached Jerusalem, they were warmly received by the church. Paul and Barnabas gave a good report of all that had happened in Antioch and along the way as they preached about Jesus and invited people to follow Him. But the Judaizers weren't mollified. They stood to their feet and insisted, "It is necessary to circumcise them and to command them to keep the law of Moses!" (Acts 15:5). The biblical record of subsequent events sounds benign, understated to say the least. "Then the apostles and the elders assembled to consider this matter. After there had been much debate . . ." (Acts 15:6). "Much debate" to be sure—what a raucous meeting that must have been! *Robert's Rules of Order* were in short supply back then. These were passionate Jewish men, skilled orators accustomed to verbal jousting to advance intellectual positions. Much debate, indeed! It's easy to imagine the intensity of the meeting since the nature of the gospel and the future of the Christian movement were at stake.

After prolonged debate Peter stood and offered some counsel based on his recent experiences. Peter reminded everyone that "in the early days God made a choice among you, that by my mouth the Gentiles would hear the gospel message and believe. . . . He made no distinction between us and them. . . . We believe we are saved through the grace of the Lord Jesus, in the same way they are" (Acts 15:7, 9, 11). Peter, whose stature in the early church was unquestioned, clearly sided with Paul in defending the gospel of grace without any human addition (even the covenant-keeping act of circumcision). Peter and Paul were unified: salvation was by faith through grace, apart from any human effort.

While Peter's speech makes it seem like he was never confused about this matter, Paul's recollection of related events paints a different picture. On a prior occasion Peter had visited Antioch and refused to eat with Gentile converts who weren't circumcised (Gal. 2:11–12). This created division in the church as other Jewish believers followed Peter's lead. Paul revealed his feelings about Peter's duplicity and how serious the problem was by concluding "the Jews joined his hypocrisy, so that even Barnabas was carried away by their hypocrisy" (Gal. 2:13). This was too much for Paul. When he saw "they were deviating from the truth of the gospel, I [Paul] told Cephas [Peter] in front of everyone, 'If you, who are a Jew, live like a Gentile and not like a Jew, how can you compel Gentiles to live like Jews?'" (Gal. 2:14). Peter, like many other Jewish leaders, struggled with circumcision and its relationship to the gospel. Paul was unflinching, however, in his defense of salvation by grace through faith alone. This confrontation between the undisputed giants of the New Testament church proves the significance of this issue and the importance of resolving it accurately.

Back in Jerusalem, Barnabas and Paul (note the order of the names in the biblical text—perhaps the more mature, cooler head prevailed) continued their report (Acts 15:12). When they finished, James proposed a solution (Acts 15:13–21), which was affirmed by the Jerusalem church (Acts 15:22). The conclusion was summarized in a letter (Acts 15:23–29) widely supported by all concerned. Paul and Barnabas along with Judas and Silas (representing the Jerusalem church) returned to Antioch with the letter and delivered their report. The Antioch church received the affirming news, reinforced by messages from the guest preachers, and then resumed their aggressive work of making disciples among the Gentiles.

What Was in the Letter?

While the Jerusalem church finally affirmed the gospel without any additions assuring its efficacy, the letter they sent to Antioch was also helpful in addressing the larger questions raised by the circumcision issue. One larger question was, What defines the requirements for Christian fellowship? Another related question was, What attitude ensures believers from different backgrounds can work together? The letter from the Jerusalem church not only preserved the gospel but also established a pattern for resolving divisive doctrinal issues among believers.

After hearing all sides of the argument, James proposed, "We should not cause difficulties for those who turn to God from among the Gentiles, but instead we should write to them to abstain from things polluted by idols, from sexual immorality, from eating anything that has been strangled, and from blood. For since ancient times, Moses has had in every city those who proclaim him, and he is read aloud in the synagogues every Sabbath day" (Acts 15:19–21). James agreed no "difficulties" should be created for new believers. He went on, however, to itemize four instructions which Gentile converts should follow to assure good fellowship with Jewish brethren. Those instructions were to abstain from anything related to idol worship, sexual immorality, strangled animals, and "from blood." The letter sent to Antioch contained those same instructions (Acts 15:29).

The letter also disavowed any official endorsement of the Judaizers ("some to whom we gave no authorization went out from us and troubled you with their words and unsettled your hearts," Acts 15:24), underscored the unanimity of everyone involved in the decision about the gospel ("we have unanimously decided," Acts 15:25), affirmed the sacrificial service of Paul and Barnabas ("our beloved Barnabas and Paul, who have risked their lives for the name of the Lord Jesus Christ," Acts 15:25–26), and attributed the final decision and the contents of the letter to the Holy Spirit's direction ("for it was the Holy Spirit's decision," Acts 15:28). The letter is conciliatory and pastoral, asking for deference from Gentile believers toward Jewish believers who had deeply ingrained ("for since ancient times . . . ," Acts 15:21) religious and cultural practices associated with worshipping God and holy living.

The four instructions in the letter addressed three issues: idol worship, sexual behavior, and food preparation. All of these, properly avoided or observed, were distinctive characteristics of Jewish religious practice. When Jews became Christians, they continued these worship and lifestyle choices as expressions of devotion to God. Two of these issues (avoiding idols and maintaining moral purity) became essential and timeless aspects of Christian discipleship (1 Cor. 10:14–22; 1 Thess. 4:3–8). Food preparation rules (particularly their relation to idol worship) changed slowly but eventually became less and less important in defining fellowship (1 Cor. 8).

The letter to Antioch asked the Gentile believers to honor these commitments as part of disciplined living. The letter also appealed for deference, making concessions to improve fellowship and working relationships among still-maturing believers. When the letter was read, the Antioch church "rejoiced because of its encouragement" (Acts 15:31). They received the letter in the spirit in which it was written and delivered. Rather than chafe under the requests, the Gentiles graciously agreed to accommodations preserving fellowship and improving their working relationship with Jewish believers. While no one was willing to compromise the gospel, everyone was willing to go the extra mile on other issues.

Stand Up and Be Counted

The battle over the nature of the gospel was a crossroads moment for the nascent Christian movement. The intensity of the debate, the arduous travel required for meetings about the issue, the high-level leaders involved, and the breadth of congregational participation by two significant churches underscores the importance of the debate at that time and for the church for all time.

The overarching lesson we learn from this story is transformational churches, and their leaders, stand for doctrinal integrity. They are willing to endure conflict, spend money to get people together to address important issues, allow (even encourage) leaders to devote time to the battle, and involve entire Christian communities in the process. When a serious doctrinal error is introduced into a healthy church, the body must mobilize to expel the antibody. A vital doctrine, in this case the doctrine of salvation, simply can't be compromised. The stakes are too high, the consequences too great. Heresy must be stopped, no matter how great the challenge or how high the cost.

The New Testament contains many instructions about the importance of preserving the unity, fellowship, peace, and harmony of a church (for example, Gal. 6:1–5; Phil. 4:1–3; Col. 3:12–17). Christians who disrupt their church for frivolous reasons must be rebuked and corrected (2 Thess. 3:6–13; Titus 3:8–11). Christians who upset their church's fellowship by sinful choices must repent or be removed if they continue to resist (1 Cor. 5:9–13). A church is supposed to be a unified, contented fellowship preoccupied with the mission of expanding God's kingdom. Every effort must be made to maintain good relationships, including doing everything possible to support struggling members and reclaim sinful rebels (Gal. 6:1–2).

Since the encouragements to preserve church fellowship and the warnings against disrupting it are both so forceful, is it ever biblically permissible to foment controversy and even divide a church? The answer, surprisingly, is yes. When a core Christian doctrine is taught erroneously, the perpetrators must be called to account, challenged to repent, resisted if they won't recant their position, and dismissed (or abandoned) if necessary. You have permission, even an obligation, to defend key doctrinal issues to this extreme.

You also have an obligation to discern the difference between "key doctrinal issues" and lesser matters that aren't worth dividing over. Further, you must develop the wisdom to know when to compromise appropriately to preserve fellowship and working relationships with other believers. Christianity, as a worldwide movement, is too complex to define one single "Christian way" for every life issue in all contexts. Cultural influences on Christianity create a vast variety among genuine believers in political persuasions, worship methods, food choices, family relationships, fellowship practices, preaching styles, and a host of other areas.

Paul, the same man who aggressively opposed circumcision as part of the gospel, soon demonstrated a remarkable deference to cultural mores on this same issue. After winning the battle in Acts 15, the narrative then reports Paul "went on to Derbe and Lystra, where there was a disciple named Timothy, the son of a believing Jewish woman, but his father was a Greek. The brothers at Lystra and Iconium spoke highly of him. Paul wanted Timothy to go with him, so he took him and circumcised him" (Acts 16:1–3). Paul, who had just fought and won a pitched battle against circumcision, immediately started his next missionary journey by circumcising a young leader before allowing him to join the missionary team.

The reason for Paul's decision was "because of the Jews who were in those places, since they all knew that his father was a Greek" (Acts 16:3). While Paul refused to circumcise anyone as part of their conversion experience (thus preserving the gospel), he circumcised a protégé in order to remove barriers to missional and ministerial effectiveness. This wasn't a repudiation of his former position because, after the circumcision, as Paul and Timothy "traveled through the towns, they delivered the decisions reached by the apostles and elders at Jerusalem for them to observe" (Acts 16:4). Paul circumcised Timothy so they could more freely preach a circumcision-free gospel.

This is a powerful example for modern Christians to emulate. We must stand for doctrinal purity while at the same time compromising on lesser (even sometimes closely connected) issues for the greater good of kingdom advance. Wisdom is required to sort out these matters. Don't expect it to be a clean or simple process. Prepare to be second-guessed and criticized by well-meaning brothers and sisters who don't see things the way you do. Nevertheless, the pattern is clear, and the responsibility can't be shirked. Some hills you die on. Some you don't. Deciding the relative importance of different issues requires Solomonic wisdom. To learn to balance defending doctrine with preserving the missional fellowship of the church, you must ask and answer one simple question.

What Doctrines Matter Most?

Some doctrines matter more than others. You may struggle with that conclusion. Yet an honest appraisal of church practices reveals it's true. For example, in my denomination, we have a confessional statement called the Baptist Faith and Message 2000.[17] It has eighteen articles or sections. The early articles are about the Scriptures, God, man, salvation, etc. Later articles cover subjects like education, stewardship, cooperation, etc. The faculty at our school must agree to teach "in accordance with and not contrary to" this doctrinal statement. When prospective faculty members are interviewed, they are always asked detailed questions about the first few articles. It is rare, however, that anyone asks much about the latter articles. Why? Because our board is more concerned the doctrines of God, Scripture, and salvation are taught accurately than they are about other issues. That doesn't mean the lesser issues are ignored (in the interview process or in our classrooms). They are simply allocated time in proportion to their perceived importance. Christians differentiate the importance of doctrinal issues. Some matters are weightier than others.

This same reality also plays itself out in practical ways in churches. When a new pastor is being considered, the doctrinal questions are usually slanted toward issues deemed most important by that congregation. Core issues, as they are determined by each church, require unanimity with any new leader. Disagreements over lesser issues may be discovered, but they usually don't disqualify candidates. Receiving members who transfer from other churches involves a similar process. Almost every church has a core set of beliefs to which its members must adhere while other issues aren't considered germane when determining membership acceptability. The point is this: almost all Christians distinguish various levels of importance between doctrinal issues. We do this intuitively based on past education, training, tradition, or experience. It's helpful, however, to be more proactive in establishing patterns for engaging these issues when considering what doctrines to defend.

In attempting to be more intentional about determining the importance of various doctrines, different strategies have been proposed, usually involving three levels or categories of theological importance. These are sometimes labeled first-order, second-order, and third-order doctrines. They can also be called primary, secondary, and tertiary doctrines. These naming strategies assume doctrinal positions can be delineated and assigned to one of these categories with first order or primary doctrines being most important. Let me add to the conversation with the following diagram.

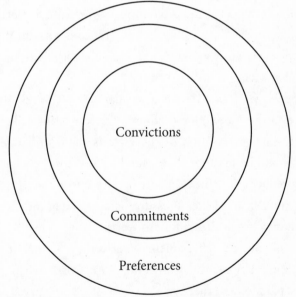

The most important doctrines in the diagram are "convictions." These are doctrines that define the Christian faith. They are nonnegotiable. They are the core of what we believe. When people deny one of these, they deny the faith. When a Christian church, denomination, or school rejects one of these, it is by definition, no longer a Christian entity. Doctrines of God (including Father, Son, and Spirit), salvation, and Scripture fall into this category (but aren't an exhaustive list). These are some of the "here I stand" convictions demarcating Christianity.

How do you know if something goes in this category? Without being flippant, the answer is these are doctrines worth dying for. Most believers in Western churches don't face this reality, but many believers around the world do. My friend John, for example, was interrogated many times while living under Communism. Several times he was asked to recant his Christian faith, under threat of death. He would not do it. He told me, "Some beliefs are too precious to compromise." Fortunately, his life was spared. But his courage has impacted me profoundly. Some truth is worth dying for, and some isn't! Knowing the difference is vital to defending the faith successfully while avoiding pointless legalistic arguments over lesser issues.

Hopefully, if faced with a similar trial, I would have the courage to die rather than compromise convictions like Jesus is the only way of salvation or the Bible is the Word of God. My prayer would be for courage to stand for certain truths no matter the consequences. While some believers encounter this kind of persecution, facing lesser pressure is more likely for most of us. These convictional doctrines are worth losing your job, walking away from your church, reducing your compensation, or severing significant relationships. Convictions are worth whatever price must be paid to hold them.

The second level of doctrinal positions is called "commitments." These are important beliefs that define believers and churches on vital issues. While they aren't "give your life" issues, they respresent commitments to positions, perspectives, and practices emerging from these doctrines. Shared commitments are the basis for local church fellowship and the practical synergy needed to do kingdom work effectively. For example, while various models of church government are permissible (with some possible scriptural foundation for each), no church will survive very long if it's members continually disagree about how to make decisions. A congregation needs a shared set of commitments about church order so decisions can be made and progress achieved.

Similarly, issues like eschatological positions, charismatic practices, and observance of church ordinances fall into this category. One positive example of such alignments in churches and groups of churches is denominationalism. Christians form churches defined by doctrinal parameters, and those churches then form denominations to work together with minimal distraction. When churches share the same "convictions" (making them "Christian" churches) and generally share the same "commitments" (uniquely defined by their doctrinal positions on second-tier issues), they are able to work together effectively.

Finally, the third level of doctrinal positions is called "preferences." These positions reflect changing tastes, regional or national biases, cultural factors, political persuasions, and generational experiences. Some might argue these aren't "doctrinal" issues at all. But they are because Christians often claim biblical (at least inferred) or traditional (historic precedent) support for these positions. For most believers, issues like dress codes (formal, informal), educational strategies (homeschool, Christian school, public school), missionary methods (independent, societal, associational), and preaching style (topical, expository) fall into this category. We have preferences based on the factors previously mentioned, but these matters don't define Christianity and aren't essential for local church or denominational effectiveness. There is wide latitude among most believers, as it should be, on many of these issues. We may not work closely together with others who don't share our preferences, but, nonetheless, we admire them and appreciate their contribution to kingdom work.

The Fundamental Challenge

Thinking through these layers of doctrinal positions—convictions, commitments, and preferences—will help you maintain doctrinal integrity in your church, denomination, or school. The fundamental challenge is identifying convictions and holding them without compromise *while at the same time demonstrating patience and grace with other believers who have differing commitments and preferences.* This is a major challenge for the church worldwide. Our failure at this task is the reason for so much rancor, bitterness, and negativity among Christians and the poor witness this gives to unbelievers.

We must develop discernment to know which doctrines matter most and stop arguing over lesser issues. While we can't compromise convictions, we must learn to tolerate (in the true sense of the word, not some politically correct aberration) other Christians with differing commitments and preferences. The secret to Christian unity isn't an institutionally or organizationally connected worldwide megachurch. The secret is being determined to separate from heretics, while loving genuine believers who differ with us on lesser issues and finding ways to work together (or at least encourage others working separately) in spite of our differences.

Oh, that this were a simple, clean, conflict-free process! But it isn't. It's messy, troublesome, and complicated. Yet the stakes are so high strong churches embrace the challenge of maintaining doctrinal integrity. They are willing to define their convictions and take them seriously. They articulate commitments their members must hold to promote fellowship and efficiency in kingdom endeavors. Transformational churches also give wide latitude, both among their membership and to the church down the street, in preferential matters. While no church does this perfectly, healthy churches do it well enough to define who they are, enable cooperative ministry, and tolerate differing opinions on issues that, in the long run, just don't matter than much.

The most explosive doctrinal conflicts occur among Christians when an issue is given more weight than it deserves, when a commitment is treated like a conviction or a preference is treated like a commitment or conviction. When this happens, we die on hills not worth the bloody battles. We defend our turf, often motivated by pride and selfishness, rather than appropriately guarding a doctrine with the level of intensity it deserves. We dissipate our influence by trifling arguments over matters made more consequential than they really are. We do this to our peril while the devil laughs at the distraction we create. Time, energy, and money are wasted that could have been spent on truly important matters. But perhaps most important, we lose credibility with a watching world. Our lack of love undercuts our message and diminishes our attractiveness to the unsaved (John 13:34–35).

Transformational churches model God's love by how they handle doctrinal matters. These churches know the difference between convictions, commitments, and preferences. Healthy churches, imperfect because of human frailty, engage this process intentionally, knowing the outcome may be messy but the results are worth the effort. Transformational churches maintain doctrinal integrity.

Questions for Reflection

1. Are you comfortable with the conclusion that doctrinal integrity trumps preserving fellowship on key convictional issues? Why or why not?

2. Which doctrinal issues are "convictions" for you? "Commitments"? "Preferences"? What are some issues you struggle to put in a category? Which issues make these doctrines difficult to categorize?

3. Which issues do Christians argue over today that just aren't that important? How can you demonstrate more patience and grace with believers who don't share your commitments and preferences?

4. What are some issues your fellow church members should compromise in order to facilitate greater kingdom advance? Are you comfortable choosing to compromise, or is "compromise" always a negative result for you?

5. On a scale of 1 to 10, how would you rate your commitment to doctrinal integrity? How about your church's commitment? What will you do to stand more firmly on doctrinal convictions?

Chapter 7

Conflict Management

A transformational church handles
conflict effectively.

Big myth: strong, healthy churches are always one big, happy family. They are devoid of conflict, always working together without tension or frustration toward mutually satisfying goals. In a dream world, healthy churches have near-perfect pastors leading unified, hardworking members through one successful ministry experience after another. When the church is envisioned as "the family of God," we imagine it resembling a perfect family, which doesn't exist any more than a perfect church does.

Most churches are like normal families—crazy uncles, bossy aunts, unruly teenagers, imperfect fathers, and overworked mothers! All families, including strong families, have conflict from time to time. That's normal when people are in vulnerable, emotionally charged relationships. In ways more realistic than idealistic, transformational churches *are* like families—normal families with occasional conflicts between people who love one another and are genuinely committed to one another for the long haul.

Another myth is mature Christian leaders never have disputes. Our incorrect assumption is pastors, missionaries, professors,

elders, and deacons have reached such a level of spiritual maturity—
evidenced by their elevation to leadership status—they no longer have
disagreements with other leaders. That's far from the truth! Leaders
aren't always perfect examples of Christian decorum. Christian
leaders—including competent, spiritually mature leaders—
experience discord with other leaders. These disagreements can be
about doctrine, methods, personnel, or personalities. Depending
on the stature of the leaders involved, in today's world these
conflicts can become media events, widely publicized and even
sensationalized beyond the true scope of their importance. These
conflicts can also result in these leaders' churches or organizations
having tension with other Christian entities.

Even when conflict is understood as a normal part of church
life, it's often assumed healthy churches handle it so well that
everyone is satisfied when it's resolved. That's another myth.
Sometimes conflict is resolved and everyone is happy with the
outcome. Other times, disagreements end with a truce, not
genuine peace. Not everyone is satisfied with the outcome and lives
happily ever after. Those conclusions end fairy tales, not real-time
divisions and debates among church members or Christian leaders.

When outsiders view strong churches from a distance, they can
have an unrealistic impression of their unity and fellowship. People
who observe Christian leaders from a distance often see only a
positive caricature. But believers closer to the situation see things
differently. Healthy churches know they have conflicts, many times
similar to the conflicts in struggling churches. Members of strong
churches still have conflict with one another and with their leaders
and observe discord among their leaders. What differentiates these
situations in healthy churches (from similar events in struggling
churches) isn't the nature of the disagreements but how they
are handled. What separates transformational churches from

dysfunctional churches is their ability to resolve conflict situations successfully and move on rather than being defined, preoccupied, or permanently entangled in the process.

First, Antioch is a model of a church handling conflict effectively. It experienced disputes over doctrinal issues, tension with another church, discord among its leaders, and division over a personnel decision. Let's look at each of these situations and their parallels in contemporary church life, along with some key principles for handling conflict in a healthy church. Remember, church health isn't defined by the absence of conflict but by how it's handled. Transformational churches manage conflict effectively.

Debating Doctrine

The conflict over the nature of the gospel was detailed in the last chapter so only a short summary is needed here, before focusing on how the conflict was handled. Antioch was a Gentile church. Some in the Jewish church in Jerusalem weren't sure about its legitimacy since people were becoming Christians without identifying with the Jewish community through circumcision. This led to a significant conflict over the nature of the gospel, whether salvation was by grace, through faith, without any human effort or addition, or by some other means. Thankfully, the true gospel was preserved but not before intense conflict over the issue was successfully resolved. How was that accomplished?

First, the issue was clearly articulated and defined. Judean leaders came to Antioch and said, "Unless you are circumcised according to the custom prescribed by Moses, you cannot be saved!" (Acts 15:1). That's definitive. One group claimed salvation was through Jesus; the other, that salvation was through Jesus plus circumcision.

Second, the issue was confronted. As we have seen in the previous chapter, this confrontation was intense and spirited. Paul and Barnabas "engaged them [the preachers from Jerusalem] in serious argument and debate" (Acts 15:2). Paul's intensity is revealed in his claim, "We did not yield in submission to these people for even an hour" (Gal. 2:5).

Third, the leaders of the early Christian movement got together to resolve the problem. Paul and Barnabas from Antioch (Acts 15:2), along with Peter, James, Judas, and Silas from Jerusalem (Acts 15:7, 13, 22), are all singled out as participants in the process. Along with these named leaders, other prominent apostles, prophets, and elders were included in the discussion (Acts 15:2, 4, 6, 22). Since travel and communication were so challenging in those days, assembling the most prominent leaders of the church for this meeting was quite a feat and illustrates the importance placed on resolving this issue.

Fourth, the leaders considered all aspects of the problem. There isn't definitive information on the length of this meeting, but it involved "much debate" from multiple speakers. It's easy to imagine it lasting for several days. However long it lasted, the leaders hammered on the issues until they reached consensus. They considered input from various perspectives before finalizing their conclusion.

They heard theological input from "believers from the party of the Pharisees," scholars who insisted it "necessary to circumcise them [the Gentile believers] and command them to keep the law of Moses!" (Acts 15:5). As former Pharisees, these men were sticklers about doctrinal detail. Their legalistic ways were deeply ingrained and colored their perspective on emerging Christian beliefs. They brought those leanings into the debate about the gospel.

The assembly also heard Peter's testimony (Acts 15:7–11) of his experience at Pentecost (Acts 2), perhaps of his vision while staying with Cornelius (Acts 10), and of his prior report to them of that experience (Acts 11:4–18). Theological input was considered, but so was the testimony and experience of this respected leader who had special insight from God. Peter's miraculous preaching at Pentecost and his vision redefining "clean" and "unclean" were germane to the discussion.

The assembly also heard missionary stories of God's recent activity among the Gentiles (Acts 15:12). Paul and Barnabas told their stories, narratives of God's saving grace revealed in Antioch and even the positive response among the Gentiles on their trip to Jerusalem for the meeting (Acts 15:3). Theological details, testimonies of God's interaction with key leaders, and stories of missionary effectiveness and gospel advance were all part of getting the facts before the assembly.

The leaders reached a consensus they (and their churches) could affirm. After all the debate—including theological input, reports of experiences with God, and stories of gospel receptivity and missional results—James proposed a solution (Acts 15:13–21). It acknowledged the observable blessing from God in so many Gentiles coming to faith, a positive acceptance of Peter's testimony (Acts 15:14), and a theological foundation based on a pertinent Old Testament passage (Amos 9:11–12, referenced in Acts 15:16–18). James wisely combined Scripture, input from key leaders, and discernment about interpreting the evidence of God's blessing to suggest his solution. His proposal preserved the gospel and at the same time preserved the fellowship of the early Christian movement. James called not only for a firm stand on an important doctrine but also for deference on lesser, yet still consequential, issues (Acts 15:19–21).

This conflict had a successful resolution, the proverbial happy ending hoped for but not always achieved. James's proposal was affirmed by the assembly and the "whole church" in Jerusalem (Acts 15:22). A letter was drafted and hand delivered by Paul and Barnabas, along with Judas and Silas representing the Jerusalem church. When the letter was read publicly, the Antioch church "rejoiced because of its encouragement" (Acts 15:31). This response was partly due to the contents but can also be attributed to the attitude with which it was delivered and the unity among the four top leaders who presented it. Christians generally want to follow their leaders, so it was probably a great relief to many when this problem was resolved so positively.

Tension between Churches

This story is also an example of conflict arising between two congregations. Jerusalem and Antioch were distinctly different churches—ethnically, politically, culturally, and geographically. Their specific conflict was over the gospel, but they could have divided over any number of other issues. Churches and ministry organizations struggle to work with other Christian groups for a myriad of reasons—some doctrinal, but often because of other issues emerging from diversity in culture, methodology, or approach.

The process to resolving these conflicts is similar to the one outlined in the previous section. Issues need to be defined, problems confronted, leaders assembled, information shared, and solutions proposed. Successful conflict resolution may lead to unity. Whether organizational or purposeful unity, open hostilities should end as a common purpose is established. When doctrinal divisions are the reason for the tension, even those mandating separation, humility and deference can still be demonstrated. Humility means holding doctrinal convictions firmly, without compromise but also without arrogance or rancor. Deference means treating other churches or groups with respect, compromising and affirming the other party when possible. While churches of differing denominations, communities, cultures, or backgrounds may not see all things the same way, they can respect one another and minimize abusive, destructive rhetoric.

Christian churches and organizations today may not always achieve the unity of Jerusalem and Antioch, but they can emulate the process and attitude that enabled the resolution of their conflict. Even when resolution means an agreement to disagree, mutual respect can still mark the encounters and even the decisions to go separate ways when necessary. Perpetual feuding that drains energy from more positive pursuits is unacceptable.

A Battle Royal

As part of the conflict about the gospel, Paul had a significant issue with Peter (and to a lesser extent Barnabas) about their behavior which contributed to the problem. While Peter claimed during the Jerusalem Council he supported Gentile conversion apart from circumcision, he had previously struggled with this and related issues. Despite his liberating vision and personal ministry among Gentiles (Acts 10), on at least one occasion Peter lapsed into legalism over the issue of table fellowship with Gentile believers.

Paul described the problem this way, "[Peter] used to eat with the Gentiles before certain men came from James [the Jerusalem church leader]. However, when they came, he withdrew and separated himself because he feared those from the circumcision party" (Gal. 2:12). This was duplicity of the highest order, behavior Paul found repulsive. But what troubled him most wasn't Peter's behavior but the scope of its influence as "the rest of the Jews joined his hypocrisy, so that even Barnabas was carried away by their hypocrisy" (Gal. 2:13).

Barnabas, Paul's mentor and companion, probably deserved a rebuke and may have received one from Paul. It's hard to imagine Paul ignored Barnabas's behavior based on how forcefully he confronted Peter. Paul wrote, "When I saw that they were deviating from the truth of the gospel, I told Cephas [Peter] in front of everyone" (Gal. 2:14). Note some of the details about this confrontation. First, Paul went after Peter on the core issue ("deviating from the truth of the gospel") not the outward expression of the problem (refusing to eat with certain people). Second, Paul confronted Peter directly and publicly. This might seem like a violation of Jesus' instructions about going to a sinning brother privately (Matt. 18:15), but it isn't. Leaders have a different level of accountability (1 Tim. 5:19–22). Public sin by a leader appropriately earns a public rebuke. Third, there is no soft-selling this conflict. It was an in-your-face, nose-to-nose, man-on-man verbal altercation.

What a conflict this must have been! Peter and Paul were the titanic heavyweights of the New Testament era. Can you hear the ring announcer in the background? "In one corner, the undisputed leader of the Jerusalem church. Over six feet tall, two hundred pounds of muscle toned by years of commercial fishing. The preacher of Pentecost and first among the Twelve—the apostle Peter. In the other corner, the unrivaled leader of the Gentile movement. Older, shorter, with body broken from suffering for the gospel. Converted terrorist, missionary, teacher, and writer—the apostle Paul." A battle royal, to be sure!

How did it ultimately end? These men dealt with the issue, resolved it, and moved on. They later cooperated and validated each other's work. Evidence of this is twofold. First, Peter made a strong statement in support of Gentile conversion at the Jerusalem Council (Acts 15:7–11). He also supported the Council's decision, both the theological and practical conclusions, and lent his considerable influence to unifying the Christian movement around the decision.

Second, and perhaps more telling about the ultimate result of this confrontation and the continuing relationship between these men is Peter's exhortation, "Regard the patience of our Lord as an opportunity for salvation, just as our dear brother Paul, according to the wisdom given to him, has written to you. He speaks about these things in all his letters, in which there are some matters that are hard to understand. The untaught and the unstable twist them to their own destruction, as they also do with the rest of the Scriptures" (2 Pet. 3:15–16). Peter called Paul his "dear brother," referenced his "wisdom," and equated his letters with "the rest of the Scriptures." Peter clearly had a profound respect and appreciation for Paul. Their public dispute didn't permanently mar, much less end, their relationship.

Christian leaders experience conflict. This dispels the myth that says discord only happens among immature, irresponsible, or carnal Christians. Peter and Paul were none of the above. They were godly men who staked their lives on and gave their lives for the gospel. They evangelized, made disciples, started and led churches, trained and appointed younger leaders, confronted culture (including powerful secular leaders), and wrote a huge part of the New Testament. Yet these same men had a public, intense dispute over the nature of the gospel and its implications.

Godly men and women have conflict in churches and Christian organizations today. To believe otherwise is embracing denial, not conflict management, as a strategy for avoiding rather than resolving differences. When Christian leaders have disputes, they can be handled effectively by following the example of Peter and Paul.

First, identify the key issue and make sure it is worth fighting over. (Remember convictions, commitments, and preferences?) Leaders, even more than other believers, must not succumb to the temptation to argue and divide over minor issues. Doing so negatively influences followers to take up frivolous causes diverting time, energy, and money from more important kingdom causes.

Second, deal with the person and problem as directly as possible. Face-to-face conversation is preferred. A video call is the next best option. A phone call will work when other venues aren't available. Avoid, in almost all circumstances, texting, e-mail, and regular mail to discuss interpersonal conflict because those communication methods make dialogue almost impossible. The most personal medium available is best when trying to resolve a conflict.

Finally, believe the best about and promote the good in other leaders. Speak and write well of them. Honor their strengths and celebrate what they do well. Leaders have many positive qualities (that's why they are chosen as leaders). They also have weaknesses because they are still human. Magnify the strengths rather than harp on the shortcomings of other leaders. When you discipline yourself to do this (and it requires real effort for most of us), you will lessen conflict and celebrate the good God is doing through others.

Choosing Sides over People

Some of the most troubling situations in churches or Christian organizations relate to conflict over personnel. Transformational churches, despite often having competent leaders, still have personnel problems. Volunteers and employees must be selected, supervised, evaluated, rewarded, disciplined, and even terminated. Leaders and fellow team members don't always see these issues the same way.

Perhaps the most well-known personnel conflict in the Bible was the argument between Paul and Barnabas over including John Mark on their missionary team (Acts 15:36–41). When Paul and Barnabas launched out on their first missionary journey, they took Barnabas's cousin Mark (Col. 4:10). He didn't last long before abandoning the work (Acts 14:13). The reason he went home is left to speculation. It might have been the arduous nature of the work. It might have been homesickness. Mark may have resented his subservient role. He may also have been frustrated with Paul's taking over as the team leader, supplanting his cousin Barnabas. Whatever the reason, Mark's tenure with the missionary team was short and his departure left a bad taste in Paul's mouth.

When it came time to leave on their second mission trip, "Barnabas wanted to take along John Mark. But Paul did not think it appropriate to take along the man who had deserted them in Pamphylia and had not gone on with them to the work" (Acts 15:37–38). The conflict was simple. Barnabas wanted to take Mark on the second journey. Paul did not. This was a conflict over missionary personnel. One leader, Barnabas, appraised Mark positively, fit for missionary service. The other leader, Paul, did not. This is a classic example of two senior leaders considering the same circumstances and character qualities but coming to different conclusions. They differed about the suitability of a person for a ministry position, for additional responsibility, and for worthiness of investment (both time and money) for future service. There was also the "family connection" overtone to the situation. Blood often is thicker than water, particularly when you are handling a conflict with a team member who is also a relative (a process fraught with unique challenges).

This difference of opinion escalated into a significant dispute. It became a "sharp disagreement" with the result Paul and Barnabas "parted company" (Acts 15:39). "Sharp disagreement" seems too soft a description of what happened. Paul and Barnabas ended their working relationship because of conflict over a personnel decision. They had shared so much together it's almost unthinkable they would divide over an issue like this.

Barnabas was Paul's sponsor (Acts 9:27–30) and mentor (Acts 11:25–26). They had already taken one mission trip together (Acts 13–14). They had stood shoulder to shoulder in both Antioch and Jerusalem for the purity of the gospel (Acts 15). Their friendship had withstood a lesser conflict when Barnabas fell under Peter's influence during the table fellowship crisis (Gal. 2:13). Paul and Barnabas were battle-hardened friends, united by their foxhole experience of shared sacrifice for the gospel. But all of that was lost over their disagreement about Mark's fitness for service. They ended their professional relationship over this issue. There's no biblical evidence they ever resumed a personal relationship either. They "parted company," apparently finally and forever.

This conflict and its results weren't confined to Paul and Barnabas. As a result of this disagreement, two other men (Mark and Silas) had to choose sides. Barnabas picked Mark and left with him on their mission trip. Paul needed a new partner and selected Silas (Acts 15:39–40). Paul and Silas had worked together previously, with Silas a key player in communicating the Jerusalem letter to Antioch. It's easy to imagine the personal struggles involved as these men sorted out their relationships and formed new ministry partnerships.

A further result of their conflict was the church at Antioch had to choose which team to support. Paul and Silas departed "after being commended to the grace of the Lord by the brothers" (Acts 15:40). There is no recorded blessing from the Antioch church for the Barnabas/Mark team. While it's risky to draw conclusions from what is *not* in the Bible, this omission seems particularly pointed. Barnabas was a beloved leader in Antioch. He had risked his reputation and jeopardized his relationship with the Jerusalem church by supporting their fledging work. The absence of any recorded commission for his new team seems like a glaring omission. The brethren commended Paul and Silas, of that we are sure. Sadly, we have no indication anything like this happened for Barnabas and Mark.

Was this the end of the story? Not quite. While Barnabas disappears from the biblical record, Mark remains a significant figure. Over the years he proved his mettle and became an important Christian leader. As Paul was concluding his final letter, he wrote, "Bring Mark with you, for he is useful to me in the ministry" (2 Tim. 4:11). The conflict between Paul and Mark was serious in the moment, but cooler heads ultimately prevailed. Mark and Paul restored their relationship, as Mark was later deemed "useful" for service. Mark also wrote a gospel, further evidence of God's blessing and his continued leadership in the early church. Whatever Mark's prior shortcomings, Paul came to value him as a leader, and he grew into a man God used in profound ways. Once again, conflict among leaders didn't permanently mar or end their relationship. Even personnel problems were solved effectively.

Handling Conflict Today

The Antioch model for handling conflict reveals some important principles and practices for churches today. Remember, however, this is only a case study. The experiences at Antioch are not exhaustive, nor should they be considered a comprehensive explanation about conflict management. Many books, Web sites, seminars, conferences, consulting ministries, and even arbitration firms specialize in resolving disputes in churches and Christian organizations. A short summary, like this one, isn't meant to minimize or oversimplify this complicated subject. Rather, by looking at the example of how the Antioch church handled conflict, some foundational principles can be learned for undergirding the process. Transformational churches will improve conflict management by applying these five principles: (1) anticipate conflict, (2) address conflict situations when they arise, (3) bring resolution to every conflict, (4) accept mixed results from conflict resolution, and (5) move on when resolution has been achieved. Let's look at each one of these principles in greater detail.

1. Anticipate conflict. Since Antioch was a healthy church and still had significant conflicts, we should assume good churches will have conflict today. Anticipating this doesn't mean we foster turmoil or stir up trouble. It also doesn't imply fatalistic dread of the inevitable. It simply means we recognize conflict happens, even in the strongest churches, and prepare for it.

Conflict occurs because we live in a sinful world, regenerate people struggle with the residue of sin, imperfect leaders make mistakes, and churches have members with varying levels of spiritual maturity. It also happens because Christians are passionate about kingdom expansion, preserving biblical fidelity, and supporting leaders they love. In addition, differences of opinion about methods, strategies, and approaches to accomplishing shared purposes may lead to disharmony. Church conflict can also happen when followers project problems at home or work into church situations. For these reasons (and probably a dozen more), conflict is inevitable. Why, then, are so many Christian leaders surprised when disagreements erupt among their followers or between them and their followers?

Wise leaders know conflict happens—it's only a matter of when and over what issues. Anticipating conflict means you prepare for it (personally and corporately) by doing some of the following.

First, study conflict management resources. Read books, attend seminars, or otherwise obtain preemptive training so you are prepared when trouble comes. Leaders should equip themselves for this challenge just as they would for handling other ministry issues.

Second, offer training on conflict resolution *when there is no significant disagreement occurring in your church or organization.* Preach on conflict stories and how they were handled in the Bible. Lead a seminar or give your leaders a book on managing conflict to read and discuss. Do this when all is calm and conflict management can be addressed without connecting it to a presenting problem.

Finally, watch the horizon and minimize potential conflict situations before they explode. Wise leaders sense trouble brewing and do their best to mitigate it. While no leader should appease people just to avoid conflict, wise leaders minimize the intensity of emerging problems. Anticipate conflict. It will happen in your church. Prepare yourself and your followers for handling it when it comes. Doing so won't eliminate conflict, but it will improve your response and increase the likelihood of a positive outcome when trouble comes.

2. Address conflict situations. The leaders in Antioch directly addressed, even confronted, conflict situations as they arose. For example, Paul and Barnabas debated the Judaizers, Paul dealt with Peter, and Paul disputed with Barnabas over Mark's future service. Most Christians, including most Christian leaders, are conflict averse. We don't like conflict. We don't want to get involved in messy situations, preferring to smooth things over and find a way to get along. Unfortunately, this strategy is often counterproductive and occasionally disastrous.

Leaders must suck up their ministerial courage, tighten their belts, and wade in where angels fear to tread. Not fun, but it's necessary! When conflict is brewing, the best response is to address the problem, not just hope it goes away. Addressing the problem, however, calls for wisdom in how to approach people, discern genuine issues, manage meetings, and communicate results. Addressing the problem doesn't mean preaching a sermon to attack anyone, taking sides on an issue prematurely, or otherwise polarizing people needlessly. A public stand on a controversial issue may ultimately be required, and should be taken courageously when necessary, but in the right way and at the right time. Too often pastors preach a solution before they understand the issues at hand, firing nuclear salvos at BB-sized problems that could have been solved more effectively through a coffee shop conversation.

Addressing conflict means you deal with protagonists directly. You discern and deal with genuine issues (not just the presenting problems), gauging the level of your response in proportion to the issues at hand. This may include one-on-one meetings, group meetings, and public comments as appropriate. In some cases it may mean using a mediator (like another church leader, a pastor from a neighboring church, a denominational leader, or a paid consultant). Wisdom is required to address conflict effectively. Unfortunately, the wisdom to do this well is often learned only through the crucible experience of doing it poorly a few times. If you have confronted conflict poorly in the past, learn from your mistakes, but don't shirk this important leadership responsibility.

Transformational churches have courageous leaders who address conflict appropriately.

3. Resolve the conflict. "Resolving" conflict may seem like too high a goal. To resolve, however, doesn't mean "to solve." To solve implies working a math problem that has an ultimate, correct, final solution. Conflicts in relationships don't often lend themselves to such precise endings. To resolve means to bring to the best conclusion possible, not end perfectly every time. What is the best conclusion possible? Based on the Antioch model, kingdom advance!

The Antioch church resolved the conflict over the gospel but accepted some deferential instructions which required wisdom and latitude to implement. Peter and Paul resolved their dispute, but not without public confrontation. Their resolution also produced division as fellow believers sided with their favorite leader. When Paul and Barnabas split up, two missionary teams formed (ultimately, a positive outcome), but apparently only one left with the church's blessing. Believers in Antioch resolved their conflicts, not always cleanly, but with the goal of getting on with Jesus' work as they understood the Spirit's leading.

The Bible, including but not limited to the Antioch example, records two possible outcomes for conflict resolution among Christians: stay and work together or separate and work apart. Ending kingdom-focused work wasn't an option. Sustaining conflict in a church wasn't an option. When ongoing conflict was present, as in Corinth, it is portrayed as an unacceptable situation to be avoided. Resolving conflict, then, leads to one of two positive outcomes. First, believers work through their issues, stay together, and get on with kingdom work. Second, believers work on their issues, separate from each other, and get on with kingdom work. These are the two options healthy Christians practice. They settle their differences and get on with the task, or they decide their problems are limiting their effectiveness and separate from each other to do better kingdom work.

Notice the conclusion to either approach: *the work of the kingdom goes on.* Perpetual conflict isn't an option. Losing focus on kingdom responsibilities and dissipating energy that could be expended in more useful pursuits is unacceptable. When staying together isn't an option, the best solution is separation for the purpose of regaining focus on evangelizing, making disciples, starting churches, and sending missionaries. Continually arguing among ourselves about who is right on a particular doctrine, issue, method, or approach is counterproductive to God's mission. Get together or move apart, but get on with kingdom work.

4. Accept mixed outcomes. While the goal of conflict resolution is kingdom advance (with the options of staying or separating always possible), the outcomes of well-managed conflict are seldom this clearly defined. A mixed result is more likely. Some protagonists will be satisfied, some mollified, and some even petrified by the process. Some who perceive they lost will silently seethe, their anger masked by spiritual platitudes and passive resistance to future initiatives. Others may claim to be satisfied while actually waiting for a future opportunity to reopen the wound when doing so will be to their advantage.

Even with a mostly positive outcome, results are often mixed. Some of the winners may suffer damaged relationships and diminished influence as a price of victory. Even when a resolution is win-win, collateral relational damage takes time to repair. Some conflict management involves compromise, particularly by leaders who may give up certain aspects of their agenda to get other items accomplished. All these mixed outcomes, though mostly positive, come with some negative baggage.

Leaders who aren't willing to accept mixed outcomes in conflict resolution are doomed to perpetual frustration. Churches are complex, people centered, relationally driven, emotionally interconnected enterprises. Pastors aren't working math problems; they are herding sheep. Conflict resolution is usually a mixed bag of positive and negative outcomes, with the overall result being kingdom advance (sometimes one baby step at a time). That's the greater good we must keep in focus as we work through thorny issues that might sidetrack our efforts. Wise leaders know when they have achieved the best resolution possible and are ready to take the next step. Wise leaders know when enough is enough and it's time to move on.

5. Move on. One of the hardest things to do in resolving conflict is accepting a mixed result and moving on. It's tempting to keep stirring the pot, hoping for the perfect outcome with everyone happy, no loose ends, and genuine appreciation for those who facilitated the process. Not likely! As we have already established, most conflicts end with a mixed bag of workable solutions and unmet expectations.

Leaders must have the discipline to say, "Enough," and move their churches or organizations forward. Moving on doesn't mean you rush ahead, bullying or bulldozing your way through sensitive issues. As a leader, you must exert maximum effort to handle discord patiently and appropriately. But being a leader also means you are wise enough to know when all that can be done has been done. Paul and Barnabas could have argued ad nauseam about Mark, and nothing would have changed. No new information would have been forthcoming, no opinions would have shifted, and no new solutions would have been proposed. At some point, to end the disagreement, one or the other of them said, "Enough," chose a new missionary partner, and moved on. Similarly, during the Jerusalem Council, James heard enough and proposed his solution. In both cases the leaders knew a perfect solution wasn't emerging, but a workable one could be found. They seized the moment and moved ahead.

Moving on doesn't mean someone has to leave, although sometimes it works out that way. To move on means agreeing on a resolution (even an imperfect one), putting the issue to rest, and shifting focus from the conflict back to accomplishing the mission of your church. Moving on is a disciplined choice to realign a church's focus, motoring toward the future rather than continuing to make pointless laps around the problems of the past.

Healthy churches experience conflict. Wise leaders anticipate conflict, address it when it happens, resolve it the best way possible, accept mixed results when necessary, and move on. Transformational churches handle conflict effectively because their leaders skillfully guide them through the process. Denial isn't a coping strategy; it's a cop-out. Determine to manage conflict and trust God to bring your church through to better days with renewed focus on kingdom endeavors.

Questions for Reflection

1. Which one of these conflicts is most troublesome for your church right now—doctrinal issues, trouble with other churches, conflict between leaders, or personnel issues?

2. What are some steps you can take to anticipate conflict and prepare your church before it happens?

3. If your church is having significant conflict right now, what steps can you take to contribute to a healthy resolution? Are you comfortable accepting mixed outcomes? Do you agree or disagree on "stay" or "separate" as viable options?

4. What does it mean to move on? Are you able to do this, or do you perpetually look for the perfect outcome? Do you have a hard time letting go of past offenses?

5. On a scale of 1 to 10, how does your church rate at handling conflict? What can you do to move the meter toward a more productive score?

Chapter 8
───────────

Leaders and Followers

A transformational church follows strong leaders.

Leadership has been the buzzword in the past twenty years for shaping corporate culture. Joseph Rost compiled a major study of the use of the word *leadership* in publications across all disciplines in the United States in the twentieth century. In publications throughout the 1980s and early 1990s, he discovered a disproportionate acceleration of the use of the word compared to other indicators describing or prescribing corporate success.[18] The number of books, journal articles, popular articles, and other publications about leadership in the last twenty years of the past century (and it doesn't seem to have slowed in this century) were staggering. Business leaders focused intently on this subject as a panacea for improving corporate performance and profitably.

It's been much the same in publications related to church growth, church development, and church health. Leadership has been the focus of many books, articles, seminars, and courses. Denominational and parachurch organizations have pioneered innovative ways to teach leadership principles to pastors and other ministry workers. Seminaries have created new courses, and even entire degree programs, in leadership. Consulting and coaching firms have emerged to train and resource church leaders. All this emphasis on leadership begs the question, *"Why."* Why put so much emphasis on leaders? If Jesus is the head of the church, the ultimate Leader, why are we so concerned with the leadership people provide?

The answer is simple: God creates, shapes, and uses strong leaders to do His work. God's pattern for accomplishing something significant, expressed throughout the Bible, usually tracks on the following path. First God allows a need. Then God calls a leader (more often leaders) to address the need. Third, God prepares the leader or leaders for the task at hand. Finally, God uses the leaders to meet the need and accomplish something significant. This is the pattern with Moses, Joshua, Nehemiah, many of the prophets, Peter, James, John, Paul, and even Jesus. God allows a need, calls a leader, trains the leader (or leaders), and then uses them to accomplish His purpose.

It's also obvious, although we often overlook this point, God actually *favors strong leaders.* He created, prepared, called, and used strong leaders repeatedly in biblical history. While he often called men who were young (David), appeared weak (Gideon), or lacked experience (Peter), by the time they stepped into the arena, they were strong men, emboldened with God's vision and power for the task at hand.

God often follows the same pattern today. When He is ready to do something significant through a church (or Christian organization), He first puts capable leaders in place. God creates, calls, shapes, and uses strong-minded, strong-willed, convictional leaders to get His work done. We shouldn't resist their contribution to churches or organizations. Some Christians, for reasons we will discuss later, are averse to strong leaders. This ignores God's pattern and prohibits us from experiencing God's best in collective efforts, guided by God-placed leaders, to achieve more than we can accomplish on our own or in a poorly led church or organization. God likes strong leaders. We should appreciate them, train more of them, and do all we can to enhance their value to the church.

Strong leaders require willing yet discerning followers to maximize their effectiveness. Being a good follower is sometimes difficult. We must learn to walk the fine line between willing submission and mindless subservience. Good leaders help their followers understand how to work with them. Good followers help their leaders by creating structures through which their almost boundless energy, gifts, and passion can be channeled. When this symbiotic relationship is in place and working well, dynamic interaction maximizing the best traits of leaders and followers (while mitigating the weaknesses of both) produces supernatural results.

Strong Leaders at Antioch

Antioch was a church with strong, capable leaders. Their most prominent leader was Barnabas. His name means "son of encouragement," and he is often portrayed fulfilling the destiny predicted by his name. He was an encourager—enabling Paul's entrance into public leadership, mentoring Mark, etc. But don't mistakenly equate his supportive demeanor with ministerial softness. Being an encourager isn't the same as being weak. Barnabas was "a good man" (Acts 11:24) of proven character and towering strength demonstrated in several incidents during his tenure in Antioch.

First, Barnabas stood up to the Jerusalem church when he affirmed the converts in Antioch and facilitated their formation into a church. The Jerusalem church originally sent him to investigate, not invigorate, the Gentile-based movement in Antioch. Instead, Barnabas assumed an ambassadorial role by appraising the situation and doing what was right for the kingdom, not what would please the constituents back home. He affirmed the Antioch believers and helped them become a functioning church. Barnabas demonstrated strength of character in this choice which he no doubt knew would be panned (or outright opposed) by the Jerusalem-based, Jewish-heritage supporters.

Second, Barnabas risked bringing Paul into public leadership. Paul was a well-known religious terrorist, complicity in Stephen's murder (Acts 7:58), and known for "ravaging the church" (Acts 8:3). After Paul's conversion, God sent him away to protect him (from others like him who stepped in to lead the persecutions) and prepare him for future service. At some point Paul needed a venue to step from the shadows into the limelight of Christian leadership and a sponsor to facilitate the transition. Barnabas had been one of the first to validate Paul's conversion and introduce him to the church at Jerusalem. When opposition to Paul's early ministry developed, he was sent to Tarsus (his hometown) both for his safety and for seasoning for future kingdom leadership (Acts 9:26–30).

Barnabas sensed it was time for Paul to reemerge in a prominent leadership role. He staked his reputation on bringing Paul to Antioch as his teaching partner. Think of the risk! What if Barnabas had been wrong? What if Paul had been a spiritual sleeper agent, a false convert biding his time and waiting for fresh opportunity to destroy the church from within? Barnabas really was "full of . . . faith" (Acts 11:24) when he made this momentous, courageous decision.

Third, Barnabas stood side by side with Paul when they confronted the Judaizers and defended the purity of the gospel

(Acts 15:2). While Barnabas did slip up, at least briefly, over the table fellowship issue (Gal. 2:13), his support for salvation by grace through faith without any human agency was clearly evident (Acts 15:2, 12). Barnabas's willingness to preach the gospel among Gentiles, even while on the way to Jerusalem to defend the gospel, is further evidence of his resolve. He was unwilling to suspend gospel-spreading activity among the Gentiles so he preached on the way to the Jerusalem Council, further risking the ire of his Jewish traveling companions accompanying him on the return trip to Jerusalem (Acts 15:2–3).

Finally, Barnabas was a courageous missionary who joined Paul on the first missionary trip (Acts 13–14) and was eager to go again until the flap erupted over Mark (Acts 15:36–41). He eventually paired with Mark and continued missionary travels. Church tradition indicates Barnabas continued in faithful ministry and later died a martyr's death. There is no reason to suspect Barnabas ever waivered in his personal faith or leadership intensity. By any definition, he was a strong leader.

Paul was another prominent leader at Antioch. To say he was a strong leader is a dramatic understatement. Paul was one of the most dynamic leaders of world history, not just first-century church history. He changed the world in his time and for all time. His conversion story is told three times in Acts (9:1–31; 22:1–21; 26:1–23) which underscores his importance in church history, even among his contemporaries. Without reviewing his entire biography, simply considering his work at Antioch is enough to demonstrate his strength as a leader.

Paul was the teacher who established the gospel among the Gentiles. He helped them understand Jesus in light of the Old Testament and created theological systems (recorded in his epistles to other primarily Gentile churches) explaining the gospel and its implications. His theological dexterity enabled him to stand up for the gospel, particularly during the Jerusalem Council, and win the day for salvation by grace through faith (Acts 15:12). Paul was also a man of action who paired with Barnabas for the first missionary journey (Acts 13–14). His record of vigorous intellectual and spiritual defense of the gospel, paired with his zealous missionary activity, demonstrates his prowess as both a theologian and a practitioner.

Paul's willingness to confront others is further evidence of his ego strength and convictional fortitude. He opposed Peter to his face in a public setting (Gal. 2:14), parted ways with Barnabas over Mark (Acts 15:39), and called the Judaizers "false brothers smuggled in" the church (Gal. 2:4). He rather indelicately wished for those so fond of circumcision to "get themselves castrated" (Gal. 5:12). Paul was a strong-minded man who wasn't afraid to let others know what he thought of them, their actions, their mistakes, and the inconsistency of their vacuous arguments.

While Barnabas and Paul were the most well-known leaders in Antioch, the Bible mentions three others by name: "Simeon who was called Niger, Lucius the Cyrenian, and Manaen, a close friend of Herod the tetrarch" (Acts 13:1). The brief biographical notes in the text about each of these men give some hint of their diverse backgrounds. Simeon, "called Niger" (meaning, *black*) may have been African, probably from northern Africa. Lucius, "the Cyrenian," may have been one of the early evangelists who helped start the church (Acts 11:20). Manean, "a close friend of Herod," is an intriguing character. The word translated "a close friend" can also mean brought up with or childhood companion. The word literally means "suckled by the same nurse." Manean had considerable social standing from his privileged upbringing as a childhood companion of a king.[19]

Three simple conclusions about leaders in transformational churches can be drawn from the Antioch model. First, a transformational church has strong leaders. Second, a transformational church has a plurality of diverse leaders. Third, a transformational church has men in leadership roles. Each of these ideas is often resisted in churches today to our detriment. Let's consider each of these principles and how they might be effectively applied today.

Strength in Leadership

The church at Antioch had strong leaders—potent pastors, elders, and missionaries who became Christian statesmen. They were convictional men, larger-than-life personalities, whose exploits shaped their generation and whose legacy shapes civilization today. They were strong willed, strong minded, spirited men. We admire them, but do we want their kind to emerge in our setting to make a similar dramatic impact? While we say yes, our actions often communicate no. Particularly as it relates to church leadership, some Christians are uncomfortable with pastors assuming too strong a role or position. Why is this true?

Strong pastoral leaders are resisted for a number of reasons, but three are particularly noteworthy today. One of these is caused by destructive leaders and their legacy. The other is a result of poor decisions by followers. The third emerges from misreading Scripture about authority structures through contemporary cultural lenses rather than as timeless truth.

First, let's consider resistance to strong pastoral leaders created by destructive leaders and their legacy. Some pastors confuse *authoritative* leadership with *authoritarian* leadership, thus creating conflict for them and trouble for the next pastor (or succession of pastors) in a church. Authoritative pastors are healthy leaders who understand the biblical parameters both for using and abusing power. They are strong leaders but demonstrate strength under control. They are under authority themselves, usually submitting to a leadership team or accountability group. Authoritative pastors are secure in their role, gentle in their use of power, and deft at shepherding their followers. They personify meekness, strength under control.

Authoritarian pastors, on the other hand, are power-hungry leaders who use their position to achieve their objectives no matter the cost to their organization or their followers. To them, people are expendable and policies aren't applicable. They bully people to fulfill their agenda rather than guide followers to implement shared commitments. They are autocratic and often communicate by word or deed, "The rules just don't apply to me." They demand of others what they aren't willing to model themselves—proper submission to authority, authority structures, organizational policies, and spiritual disciplines.

These pastors are abusive leaders guilty of ministerial malpractice. They mangle people emotionally and hurt people spiritually. They poison their followers' perspective on pastoral leadership and make it exponentially harder for the next person to do an effective job. When Christians are subjected to this kind of spiritual abuse, they rightly reject it and any semblance of so-called "leadership" they perceive to be anything like it in the future. The legacy of these dysfunctional, pseudo-leaders can take years to overcome as the wounds of spiritual abuse heal slowly. As a result of these poisonous relationships, some Christians reject any semblance of pastoral authority—tossing the baby out with the bathwater, so to speak. When this happens, the value of legitimate, authoritative pastoral leadership is diminished or lost.

Second, resistance to strong leaders also emerges from poor

decisions by followers in their relationship to and understanding of leadership, even healthy leadership. Strong leaders are sometimes resisted because they threaten existing power bases in churches, pet projects or ministries some members don't want changed, and sinful behavior some believers want ignored. Believers use these self-serving reasons to justify resistance to pastoral leaders having authority over them. Unfortunately, the church landscape is littered with the corpses of congregations that have made this choice.

When a leader faces this kind of resistance, "thus says the Lord" prophetic speaking must be coupled with calculated courageous decisions affirming "even if He does not rescue us, . . . we will not serve your gods" (Dan. 3:18). Confronting entrenched carnal Christians who are guarding unholy turf, manning outdated ministry programs, or masking secret sin is painful—but necessary. Like a physician opening an infected wound, the stench may be noxious. Inflicting pain, and having it inflicted in return, may be the only path to ultimate healing. The fight may be intense . . . and a leader may lose. Yes, read that again if you are a church leader. *You may lose.* But leaders know God has called them to do the right thing, not take the easy path. Strong leaders confront followers who resist authoritative leadership for self-preserving, kingdom-limiting reasons. Followers prejudiced against strong leaders because of self-absorbed, sin-defending resistance to change limit God's work and must be overcome. Paul's sarcastic wish for the "circumcision party" to experience castration (Gal. 5:12) illustrates the depth of his disdain and aggressiveness of his opposition to these misguided believers. There was nothing soft or subtle about his approach. Sometimes direct confrontation is necessary.

This leads to the third reason some followers reject strong leaders, misreading Scripture passages about authoritative leadership through current cultural lenses rather than as timeless truth. Part of the issue is the infiltration into churches of the general rejection of authority in modern life. God affirms authority structures in the home (Eph. 5:22–6:4), community (Rom. 13:1–7), and church (Eph. 4:11–16). God works through these structures to give order, guidance, and protection to society in general and his people in particular. Rejecting these structures invites chaos. Misusing them oppresses and abuses people. Living in harmony with these structures produces balance and blessing. Denying their existence, however, undermines the timeless truth of God's societal order and robs us of the blessing of living safely, securely, and without fear.

God expects church leaders to understand authority and use it appropriately in leadership relationships (Matt. 20:20–28). God also expects followers to submit to healthy leaders, working cooperatively with them (Heb. 13:7). At the core of this relationship, for both leaders and followers, is the bedrock conviction God is ultimately in charge. Pastoral leaders draw appropriate authority from God and are accountable to Him for how they use their power. Followers trust God to work through their leaders to direct them to heights of spiritual experience they would not likely achieve on their own. Both followers and leaders find instruction and caution in the command to "obey your leaders and submit to them, for they keep watch over your souls as those who will give an account, so that they can do this with joy and not with grief, for that would be unprofitable for you" (Heb. 13:17).

Can the relationship among leaders and followers become destructive and unhealthy? Do leaders sometimes become autocratic, drifting from authoritative to authoritarian leadership? Do followers sometimes resist, not when it is appropriate (as we will discuss later in the chapter) but simply to assert their will and stymie God's progress? Absolutely *yes* to all! Yet, despite the potential for abuse rooted in the shared sinfulness of leaders and followers, applying God's design for leadership structures in the church is still a better strategy than creating alternative models. The alternatives, similarly tainted with sin, will also lack the promise of success that comes when God's ideal is at least approximated (even when not fulfilled perfectly).

Another culturally influenced factor is resistance to strong pastors because of contemporary misperceptions of how they should be lead. Pastors in the Bible were men of conviction and action (like Barnabas, James, Titus, and Timothy). Some believers today want pastors to be sweet fellows who dress nicely, talk softly, and smile sweetly. They should be gentle souls who care for everyone, keep the peace, and avoid controversy. While that may be a modern model, it's far from a biblical ideal. Pastors are supposed to be men—real men—who represent God's love and holiness, His mercy and wrath on sinners, His forgiveness and judgment of sin, and His consolation and discipline of believers. In the description of early church leaders, they often "stood up" (for example, Acts 11:28; 15:7) when speaking on important subjects. That simple descriptor reveals more than body language. It's a literary clue to the intensity, boldness, and courage of leaders willing to stand up and be counted.

God's plan is for strong leaders to work through appropriate structures to benefit their followers. While strong leaders are evident in Antioch, something gave balance. Something channeled their strength and kept them from running amok. Strong leaders have strong personalities, preferences, and peccadilloes. They have quirks, mannerisms, catch phrases, and pet subjects. They are persuasive, often verbally gifted, and capable of winning the day in almost any debate. It's easy for them to get off track. As a person once told me, "Jeff, even when you are wrong, you sound right." That's a dangerous talent to have!

Did the church at Antioch have a perspective or a practice that unlocks the secret to balancing strong leaders? Is there a pattern or principle that keeps leaders authoritative without allowing them to drift into sinful patterns of authoritarian leadership? The answer is yes, and it's so obvious it's easy to read over it quickly and miss it entirely.

Leading Together

The strong leaders in Antioch worked, in every recorded case, in partnerships or in a team environment. When the Antioch church began, it started with "some . . . Cypriot and Cyrenian men" (Acts 11:20), not one man but *men* who shared the gospel and started the church. After the church grew rapidly, Barnabas was sent from Jerusalem to check out the movement. He arrived, surveyed the situation, and immediately left town to retrieve Paul (Acts 11:25). Barnabas chose a partner before he initiated the work of turning the early converts into a functional church.

When the church assembled for worship, multiple worship leaders were prominent in the service (Acts 13:1). They were an interesting collection of multicultural, multiethnic believers. The leadership team reflected the diversity of the Antioch church, which had emerged from the cosmopolitan population of the city. The church had a recognized, representative team of men who guided them in worship and decision making (Acts 13:2).

When Barnabas and Paul were set apart and sent out on the first mission trip, they were sent together (Acts 13:3). They stayed together through the first trip and were preparing to make a second trip when the trouble erupted over Mark. When that was settled, notice what happened next (Acts 15:36–40). Two new partnerships replaced the original pair. Both Paul and Barnabas chose a new teammate rather than launch out as solo missionaries.

My church planting experience was a team effort. My friend, Joe Flegal, was a true partner. We worked side by side for many years to establish a new church. A few years later, while reminiscing about the early days, I told Joe, "You know, there were some days the only reason I went to the office was I knew you would be there. You kept me going." He laughed and replied, "Well, some days, the only reason I went to work was I knew you were there and so I had to show up." Working alone, it's doubtful we would have endured. Working together, we were instrumental in establishing a thriving church.

When it was time for theological debate, Paul and Barnabas went to Jerusalem together, along with a team of other leaders (Acts 15:2). They took on the Judaizers, standing together for the gospel (Acts 15:12). When the Jerusalem Council decision was finalized, Paul and Barnabas (along with Judas and Silas from Jerusalem) formed the team that delivered the news back to Antioch (Acts 15:30–35).

In every case in Antioch, the leaders worked in partnerships or teams. There's no question Paul and Barnabas were prominent leaders, strong leaders by any definition. But the strength of their personalities, convictions, and passions was evened out by working with other leaders of similar strength. The pattern in Antioch was leadership partners or leadership teams. No one led alone.

Throughout Acts this pattern continued. With rare exception (like Paul in Athens, one of his least productive mission sites, Acts 17:16–34), the missionaries and other early church leaders worked in pairs or groups. The "we" passages of Acts are more than an inclusion of the author in the story line. They underscore

Paul and his team traveled, lived, and worked together. Later, when Paul started appointing church leaders, he appointed "elders," not *an* elder, to church leadership roles (for example, Acts 14:23). Throughout the New Testament the predominant model was a plurality of leaders sharing church leadership responsibilities.

The secret to maximizing the impact of strong pastors is the tempering effect of working in a team environment. While a pastor is the "leader of equals," there still must be a sense of deference among the leadership team that keeps any one personality, opinion, or persuasion from dominating the decision-making process. Contrary to the fears of some, capable leaders are actually made stronger, not weaker, by working in a team environment. Bad ideas and potential mistakes are filtered before they reach a public audience, therefore making the primary leader and the leadership team more effective in the eyes of their followers. Like a good theatrical director, a leadership team deletes the worst scenes before the show goes public. In addition, when a controversial, difficult, or radical idea comes forward with a team's endorsement and support, it has more legitimacy for followers who know "plans fail when there is no counsel, but with many advisers they succeed" (Prov. 15:22).

A church (or any Christian organization) needs strong leaders. Strong leaders need a team (deacons, elders, trustees, executive cabinet, board members, leadership council, etc.) around them for balance and perspective. This kind of effective team is more than a collection of sycophants or yes-men. It must be a team of equals, working collaboratively, committed to consensus decisions on matters of preference, and determined to ask one another hard questions leading to intentional, mission-driven decisions. This is the secret to getting the best contribution from strong leaders while also mitigating the sinful tendencies of overbearing egos. Ask

God for strong-willed, quick-minded, action-oriented, definitive, decision-making leaders for your church or organization. Then insist they work in the checks and balances of a team environment. Doing so ensures the best leadership possible, balancing the drive of strong leaders with the collective insight of wise counselors. If you are currently a solo leader, take the initiative to develop and participate in a team leadership environment. Remember, even the Lone Ranger had Tonto!

The pattern at Antioch was this: strong leaders worked in a team environment. Strong leaders are necessary. They keep churches moving forward, taking risks, attempting faith-requiring ventures, resisting doctrinal error, and demanding membership integrity. Strong leaders challenge lethargy, make tough decisions, and motivate people to accomplish together what they never would have dreamed by themselves. Put those dynamic leaders in a team environment, and these positive qualities are only accentuated.

Strong leaders, if they operate without appropriate restraint and accountability, can be destructive. Their dreams can exceed available resources. Their zeal can make people seem expendable. Their sense of urgency can angrily drive people away rather than shepherd them forward. Strong leaders can devolve destructively unless they are balanced by working in partnerships or in a team environment. Balancing individual strength with team accountability creates the best possibility for dynamic progress. The Antioch model, so simple yet so effective!

Men in Church Leadership

As if the preceding few pages weren't controversial enough, let's now go where angels fear to tread—the issue of gender in church leadership roles. At Antioch the named leaders of the church were all men. This is striking given the prominence of women in Jesus' ministry and their significant role in the church throughout Acts. What does the Antioch model mean as an example for church leadership?

Put most directly, the Antioch model demonstrates transformational churches have men in prominent leadership roles. This does not exclude, ignore, or demean the contribution of women. It simply underscores this pattern: strong churches have men who take the lead.

Practically speaking, most pastors know churches with men in visible leadership roles attract other men and inspire them to Christian service. They also know most men are not led to faith through their wife or children. It usually works the other way. When a man is converted, his wife and children usually follow in short order. Prioritizing men in leadership doesn't diminish the value of women. It simply recognizes the practical reality in most cultures: when men lead, other men, women, and children will follow.

Jesus liberated women from religious and cultural oppression, giving them spiritual status equal to men. Paul underscored this by concluding, "There is no Jew or Greek, slave or free, male or female; for you are all one in Christ Jesus" (Gal. 3:28). Encouraging women in Christian service follows Jesus' example and applies Paul's conclusion. The prominence of male leaders at Antioch doesn't discount the contribution of women (or mean there were no women in significant roles in Antioch). It only magnifies the importance of men taking the point in church leadership.

The more significant problem in most churches today isn't the absence of women in leadership; it's the declining number of men who will lead. Calling for men to fulfill their biblical responsibility as spiritual leaders doesn't diminish the role of women. It simply challenges men to do their part. The church needs both men and women in leadership. Women are often willing to serve. It's the men who are lagging!

The Antioch model doesn't solve all the dilemmas related to gender-specific roles and responsibilities in church leadership. The information provided in the textual record (our specific case study) is too limited to answer all gender-related questions about church leadership roles. Work on these issues has spawned a shelf of books on the subject! Detailing all the arguments is far beyond the scope of our case-study approach. Clearly, however, the named leaders at Antioch were men, an important fact that can't be ignored.

The focus here, then, is on creating strategies to emulate that pattern. Prioritizing men in leadership is not difficult but requires intentional effort in a contemporary culture that devalues masculinity. Here are a few suggestions on developing men as more prominent leaders in local churches.

First, design worship services and other church activities with men in mind. While planning worship services, for example, choose a representative man in your church and evaluate the level of participation that activity or event will likely elicit. While I was serving as a pastor, we selected Sonny for this purpose. He was middle-aged, committed to the Lord and the church, owned a small construction company, had younger adult children and a grandchild or two. We often asked, "Will Sonny sing this?" when selecting songs for the Sunday services. We asked, "Will Sonny do this?" when planning different worship elements or creative ways to do things like baptism or the Lord's Supper. While Sonny wasn't the only representative person we used during worship planning, it was important to have a representative man (along with women, teenagers, and children) in mind during our planning processes. If worship services aren't designed with men in mind, they aren't likely to participate, much less lead them. The same is true for other church activities.

Second, train men to lead in public settings and communicate the expectation they will take the lead in the church. During my first pastorate, for example, we made a list of every male resident member of the church. We then worked through the list, asking men to fulfill the simple responsibility of leading a prayer during a worship service. We had about two hundred men on the list, with four to six prayers in worship services each weekend. We determined not to ask anyone to pray twice before all had been asked to pray once. The results were amazing and surprising. Some men, we discovered, had never prayed in front of anyone, not even their family. When asked to pray at church, they often initially declined. But we weren't so easily dissuaded. We asked if we could help them write a prayer they could deliver in the service. This turned into a teaching moment and an occasion of significant growth for many. We also had men who were convicted of sin, shortcomings, and coldheartedness just through the request to pray in a worship service. In several instances men declined to pray and then later came by my office to talk about why they had refused. Sins were confessed, hidden struggles revealed, and spiritual growth happened because of this simple process.

Third, create a process for men to train men for leadership. This can take many forms. One pastor of a large church chooses about two dozen men each year to meet with him each Friday morning for Bible study, leadership development, and mentoring in ministerial functions. These men consider it a high honor to spend this time with their pastor. Each year the pastor chooses a new group and, over a long tenure, has personally trained several hundred men. They became the deacons, teachers, officers, and workers the church needed to continue enlarging its ministry over time.

Another pastor initiated a one-on-one process to train men for leadership. He met with each man for three to six months, working through a prescribed curriculum. The men he mentored made a commitment to doing the same for at least one man when they had completed their time with the pastor. The pastor usually met with one or two men per week, on a rotating basis. While the results were slow in the beginning, after a while, several dozen men in the church were meeting with and mentoring other men as leaders.

Fourth, develop some ministries that are "just for men." These can take different forms based on the church's setting and the interests of the men involved. One church in Idaho has a two-week hunting camp every fall for its men (also open to men in the community). The camp is set up in the wilderness and manned by the pastor and a few other churchmen. As guys hunt for a few days during that two-week time frame, they cycle through the camp for evening Bible study, prayer, and fellowship. This bonding experience has produced a cadre of men with deep relationships who are the rock-solid core of a good church. Other churches sponsor men's retreats, golf tournaments, wild-game dinners, car shows, and other events "just for men." These gender-specific events not only train and build fellowship among "the guys" but also send a clear message that men matter to the church.

Fifth, develop ministries for men to impact boys. Young men have an innate craving for the attention, approval, and blessing of older men, particularly their fathers, but also from older men they respect in general. Churches with men in leadership recognize the need to mentor young men toward leadership. While some activities should be for men only, others can be expanded to include young men and boys. Doing this creates opportunities for modeling the Christian faith, experiencing the Christian life from a manly perspective, and communicating the expectation of becoming future leaders to those who experience these events. It is vital for boys to see men modeling prayer, Bible study, Christian service, and church leadership if they are to grow into leaders for the future.

When Not to Follow

This emphasis on strong leaders and willing followers raises the question, "Is there ever a time *not* to follow?" While there's no example of the church at Antioch rejecting its leaders, there are examples of their leaders refusing to follow the Jerusalem church leaders. There are two broad categories of instances when a Christian should—in fact, *must*—refuse to follow the direction of spiritual leaders no matter how prominent, experienced, unified, or confident their decisions.

Christians must reject leaders who promulgate doctrinal error. The conflict over circumcision related to conversion is a good example. Paul was unwilling to compromise the gospel and rejected the preachers from the Jerusalem church who taught this error (Acts 15:2). Believers must also confront behavior that compromises church fellowship. Paul confronted Peter over the issue of his refusing table fellowship with uncircumcised Christians (Gal. 2:14). Doctrinal error and church damaging behavior are two examples of instances when leaders must be legitimately resisted. Being a good follower means affirming and supporting strong leaders in every way possible but not following them blindly. Transformational churches follow strong leaders but also have the fortitude to stand up to them when their behavior requires correction.

Questions for Reflection

1. How do you define strong Christian leadership? Who are some good examples of the best church leaders you have ever followed? What made them so remarkable?

2. Have you had a bad experience with a church leader? What happened? What effect has that experience had on your responsiveness to other church leaders?

3. What is your church's practice of mentoring men for leadership? Does it need to become more intentional? How?

4. Have you ever resisted your church's leaders? Why? Did you handle the situation appropriately? If not, what will you do differently next time you face a similar situation?

5. On a scale of 1 to 10, how effectively does your church practice a partnership or team leadership model? What would need to change to implement a more collaborative model?

Chapter 9
_____

Generous Sacrifice

A transformational church gives itself away.

God's economy for individuals and churches is based on giving, not getting. That's counterintuitive and countercultural but true nevertheless. Giving away resources, not hoarding them, opens the channel of God's blessing and assures adequate flow from His abundant provision. God prospers individuals and churches that are generous with their resources including time, personnel, and money. Jesus said, "Give, and it will be given to you; a good measure—pressed down, shaken together, and running over—will be poured into your lap. For with the measure you use, it will be measured back to you" (Luke 6:38). While that promise is made in the context of granting and receiving forgiveness, the principle has broader application. Jesus used the analogy of a basket being filled with grain, a good measure. When it seemed full, the grain could be pressed down and shaken together, thus increasing the amount the basket could hold. Jesus taught generous givers will be replenished like that grain basket. They will have so much their container will run over!

Paul echoed a similar theme when he wrote, "Remember this: the person who sows sparingly will also reap sparingly, and the person who sows generously will also reap generously. . . . And God is able to make every grace overflow to you, so that in every way, always having everything you need, you may excel in every good work" (2 Cor. 9:6, 8). Generous giving begets generous provision from God. Paul continued the agricultural metaphors when he wrote, "Now the One who provides seed for the sower and bread for food will provide and multiply your seed and increase the harvest of your righteousness, as you are enriched in every way for all generosity, which produces thanksgiving to God through us" (2 Cor. 9:10–11).

Church leaders give many excuses for ignoring these principles and being selfish with resources. Some say, "When our church is larger, we will give more." Others believe, "We are a small church. The big churches should be the generous givers." Many leaders promise, "We need to take care of our needs right now. We will give more someday." Another oft-heard comment is, "We need to build home base so we can give to missions and other causes later." While these statements sound reasonable, they are more folklore than fact.

Transformational churches are generous with their resources. They give themselves away. They give when they are struggling with ministry challenges, faced with many local needs, and when it's economically difficult. They give out of conviction, believing God will honor them for their generosity and meet any needs created by their giving. The church at Antioch modeled generosity. It was a young church with compassion for others and passion for spreading the gospel. Those convictions expressed themselves in tangible gifts of money and people that are an example for strong churches in every generation.

Antioch Gave Away Its Money

The first noteworthy offering in the church at Antioch was in response to an appeal from a guest preacher, Agabus. He was among some "prophets [who] came down from Jerusalem" (Acts 11:27). Agabus was a well-known preacher in the early church. He later delivered the message to Paul, warning him about the trouble awaiting him in Jerusalem, which would lead to Paul's arrest and lengthy imprisonment (Acts 21:10–11). His message to Antioch was simple: famine was coming, and relief funds were needed in Judea (Acts 11:28).

When the Antioch church heard this message, they immediately responded as "each of the disciples, according to his ability, determined to send relief to the brothers who lived in Judea. This they did, sending it to the elders by means of Barnabas and Saul" (Acts 11:29–30). This seems like such a simple story until you consider the rest of the story.

The context for the offering is significant. The Jerusalem church had been given the gospel and told to share it with the whole world (Acts 1:8). They had experienced Pentecost; the inauguration of the gospel movement evidenced by believers speaking in multiple languages so people from many nations could be saved (Acts 2:1–4). Despite these clear instructions and supernatural interventions, the Jerusalem church did *not* aggressively share the gospel among the Gentiles. For several years after Pentecost, the church kept the gospel in Jerusalem, sharing it among the Jews and building a Jewish-oriented church. While the gospel was occasionally shared with a Gentile (like the Ethiopian eunuch, Acts 8:26–40), the church remained a predominantly Jewish movement in its early years.

When the gospel finally exploded from its Jerusalem-imposed shackles, it did so only as a result of persecution and the forced scattering of believers (Acts 8:4; 11:19). Fortunately, some men boldly shared the gospel, and the first large-scale preaching among the Gentiles resulted in the founding of the Antioch church (Acts 11:19–21). The Jerusalem church grew concerned about those developments and sent Barnabas to check out the events in Antioch (Acts 11:22). He surveyed the situation, surmised God was at work, fetched Paul, and set to work transforming the converts into a congregation (Acts 11:23–26).

In that context Agabus appealed for a relief offering. He asked the Gentile Christians at Antioch to give to Jewish believers who had withheld the gospel from them, cast doubt on the authenticity of their conversion, and sent an outsider to verify the legitimacy of their church. Imagine if a church from another denomination attacked your church, questioned your faith, publicly criticized your ministry efforts, and then sent one of their pastors to ask you for a relief offering to help them recover from a natural disaster! How would your church likely respond?

While some churches might resist giving in these circumstances, the Antioch church did not. They sent money to the famine victims, not holding their previous behavior against them. Hungry people needed help. That fact trumped everything. The Antioch Christians gave willingly to assist fellow believers, even those they might have resented. This is a remarkable story of love overcoming divisions among believers to meet a pressing need.

It's also a story of churches overcoming doctrinal tensions to work together. The conflict about the gospel between these two churches has already been described in previous chapters in this book. The Jerusalem and Antioch churches had significant differences requiring extensive efforts to resolve controversial issues. In the context of this simmering conflict, Agabus arrived and asked for an offering. The Antioch church overcame its theological tension with Jerusalem and responded favorably. The overriding issue of human suffering, hungry famine victims, overcame doctrinal division and prompted unified action.

Maintaining doctrinal distinctions is essential, and theological positions should be appropriately defended (see chapter 6). These differences can be set aside, however, to meet critical needs. Love demands action during a crisis. Tornadoes, hurricanes, tsunamis, earthquakes, or other natural disasters create famine, nakedness, homelessness, and other forms of human suffering. When these things happen, the love of Jesus Christ compels every church to take action to help all people including members of other churches or religions with which we may have significant differences. Doing this doesn't compromise our beliefs. Jesus said it validates them in the eyes of a watching world who "will know that you are My disciples, if you have love for one another" (John 13:35).

At Antioch, "each of the disciples, according to his ability, determined to send relief" (Acts 11:29) to Judea. This offering wasn't given out of the surplus of a few wealthy members. It was a widespread effort of shared sacrifice. The Antioch Christians gave according to their ability or in proportion to their resources. Generous churches are made up of individuals willing to sacrifice so their church can, in turn, make a corporate impact with its giving.

Antioch Gave Away Its Leaders

Most Christians expect their church to be generous with its money. They expect their church to use its financial resources to build its ministry and also bless others. Giving away money is one way a church demonstrates generosity. The Antioch church gave away its money. But it also gave away something far more valuable. The Antioch church gave away its best leaders.

The believers gathered for worship at Antioch in a service that would change their world and ours. Barnabas, Paul, Simeon, Lucius, and Manaen—their "prophets and teachers"—were directing the service. "As they were ministering to the Lord and fasting, the Holy Spirit said, 'Set apart for Me Barnabas and Saul [Paul] for the work that I have called them to.' Then, after they had fasted, prayed, and laid hands on them, they sent them off" (Acts 13:2–3).

The Holy Spirit intervened in the worship service with unusual directions: send Barnabas and Paul as missionaries to other places. We usually think of God's call coming directly to its recipients. While that is a common pattern, it wasn't the case in this worship service. Note carefully the text, "The Holy Spirit said, 'Set apart for Me Barnabas and Saul.'" The Spirit prompted fellow believers to tell Barnabas and Paul they were being called to missionary service.

It might have happened like this. A person stood up during the worship gathering and said: "I have an unusual idea. I think it's from the Lord. Paul and Barnabas, you are supposed to leave us and take the gospel to other Gentile cities." Then another person said, "That's the same impression I'm having." A third spoke up: "You won't believe this, but those thoughts have also come to my mind. I was praying just now if I should speak up." It may not have happened exactly like that, but then again it might have! That kind of congregational participation is implied in the text. No recipient of the message is identified: only the Source is identified and emphasized. The Spirit gave Paul and Barnabas a third-party call to missions.

Paul and Barnabas received the message as from the Spirit and soon left on the first intentional mission trip in church history. Antioch sent its best leaders to carry the gospel to new cities, plant new churches, make disciples in new places, and later appoint elders in those churches. The church sent 40 percent of its named leadership team to minister in other locations. The case could be made, based on the prominence of Paul and Barnabas in the Antioch narrative, that they sent away their most capable 40 percent.

Churches today are usually willing to send members on mission trips or short-term assignments to neighboring congregations. They encourage youth groups to make these trips and younger ministers to answer these calls. They don't usually assume, however, their senior leaders will be the first to go. Not the Antioch church. They determined to start a significant missionary movement by sending their most experienced leaders to do the job. Their generosity in sending their best leaders is another example of their giving whatever was required to meet the opportunities God presented.

The results of their efforts were dramatic. God fulfilled His promise to bless a generous church with overflowing results. New churches were born (on the first mission trip, Acts 13:4–14:28) in Salamis, Paphos, Pisidian Antioch, Iconium, Lystra, and Derbe. At other preaching points along the way, people heard the gospel, and perhaps other unnamed churches originated. Later, after Paul and Barnabas separated, the work continued with the blessing and support of the Antioch church (Acts 15:40). The second mission trip (Acts 16:1–18:22) resulted in new churches in Philippi, Thessalonica, Berea, Athens, Corinth, and Ephesus. The influence of the Antioch gift of their best leaders continued to overflow with God's blessing of new churches across the Middle East and Asia Minor. Finally, on the third missionary journey (Acts 18:23–21:14), Paul and his team further strengthened the existing churches as well as planted gospel seeds in various new locations. While it's not traditionally numbered as a mission trip, Paul also took the gospel to Rome, the center of the Roman Empire (Acts 28:14). All this happened because of the spiritual sensitivity and obedience of the Antioch church.

The gospel spread across the Mediterranean world, churches were started in major cities, the Christian movement gained an irrevocable foothold among Gentiles (still flourishing today), and the framework for the Pauline epistles (written to instruct early churches) was established—all because Antioch gave away its best leaders. Jesus' promise of "a good measure—pressed down, shaken together, and running over" was fulfilled through Antioch. Their generosity cemented their preeminence in church history as the model church for maximum missional impact. Their basket has certainly overflowed!

Applying these principles is essential in building a transformational church. Creating a generous church willing to give away its resources, people and money, isn't easy in contemporary culture. Greed, materialism, egocentric leadership, selfishness, short-sightedness, the prosperity pseudo-gospel, and a general lack of faith God will provide all work against developing a disciplined commitment to congregational giving. In the face of these obstacles, how do you build a generous church today?

Develop Stewards

In a relatively short period of time, the Antioch believers progressed from new converts to sacrificial givers. How did this happen? Acts offers no detailed answer but hints about how the process might have unfolded. Paul and Barnabas taught the church "for a whole year" (Acts 11:26). No curriculum is described or prescribed. Possible content of their teaching can be surmised, however, from later events recorded in Acts. Paul and Barnabas must have taught the gospel, its implications, and its nuances. They taught the new believers how to distinguish doctrinal error and stand for the truth. That's clear from the support the Antioch church gave them in opposition to the Judaizers. They probably taught the mission imperative of the gospel and a church's responsibility to start other churches—hence, the genesis of the church planting movement through Antioch. It's easy to assume these subjects were part of the curriculum based on the later actions of the Antioch church. Instruction, not spontaneous insight, made these realities part of their newfound Christian faith.

Continuing this line of thought, it's also probable Paul and Barnabas taught the Antioch believers about financial stewardship. They might have taught them God owns everything and has shared some of His resources with them, so they were responsible to give a generous portion back to God for His work and then to use the balance of His provision wisely. These are benchmarks of Christian stewardship. Their readiness to donate, demonstrated in their response to Agabus' appeal, makes clear the Antioch Christians had been taught to give. Their disciplined giving, "each . . . according to his ability" (Acts 11:29), is further evidence of having learned the principles of proportional giving. God expects equal sacrifice, not equal gifts, from His people. This principle is rooted in the biblical concept of tithing, giving 10 percent of one's gross income for kingdom purposes. Remember, these Gentile believers were not necessarily familiar with the Old Testament and would not have known God's pattern of proportional giving without instruction by someone (like Paul) familiar with the concept. It's plausible, therefore, to conclude stewardship was one of the subjects taught to Antioch believers in their first year as a church.

One of the mistakes church leaders make is not teaching stewardship as a continuing, core component of the disciple-making process. Too many pastors focus on fund-raising as the solution to their church's financial needs. That's not the biblical pattern or solution. The key to building a generous church is systematically, routinely, and repetitively teaching stewardship. This includes biblical foundations as well as practical applications like personal/family financial management, giving responsibilities and methods, saving for future needs, and estate planning. Excellent products exist to support any church with a commitment to maintain a comprehensive stewardship discipleship program. Stewardship should be taught, must be taught, and is relatively easy to teach. So, why isn't it being done?

First, some pastors are afraid to talk about money-related issues. They fear offending people, particularly non-Christians, who hear them speak on these subjects. People *are* often offended by repeated, urgent, guilt-laden appeals to give, give, give. They aren't usually offended by a responsible, comprehensive presentation of biblical truth about money; and if they are, that reveals a deeper problem! Greed is rampant in the American church. Most surveys indicate American evangelicals give about 3 percent of their income to support kingdom endeavors. That's deplorable! Yet many leaders still refuse to speak on these issues. They are willing to preach on sexual behavior and orientation, gender roles and responsibilities, and environmental and political concerns but refuse to address blatant greed. Their real issue isn't fear of what other people will think. It's the lack of fear of a holy God and courage to address materialistic excesses in both church and culture.

Second, some leaders can't teach stewardship because they don't practice it. You really can't preach what you don't practice. When a Christian leader, for example, doesn't live on his income, give away more than a tithe, save for future needs, or have an estate plan, it's impossible to teach others to do so. Practicing Christian stewardship is a mark of maturity. No person is fit for Christian leadership, certainly not for senior leadership, who isn't practicing biblical stewardship principles.

Third, some church leaders want a quick fix, not a long-term solution, to financial challenges. They go from one fund-raising crisis to another, hoping money will somehow be found for each project or need. This approach often works well the first time, with diminishing results each time it's repeated. A better approach than fund-raising is building stewards. One retired pastor who had successfully led three churches to become financial dynamos was asked at a conference, "How did you raise so much money throughout your ministry?" He replied, "I never raised any money. I grew stewards." He taught stewardship routinely and systematically. People grew slowly but steadily into wise managers and generous givers. Over time their giving grew into a crescendo of resources amply supplying church needs and generously giving to mission projects, building programs, and other causes. Developing stewards takes time, but it's time well spent investing in the long-term financial health of individuals, families, and ultimately churches and kingdom enterprises.

Finally, some leaders plan to teach stewardship (someday) but only as an advanced course in Christian discipleship. The Antioch model shows teaching people how to manage money and give it away is part of basic training, not graduate school. When we started our church in Oregon, our early converts often had little or no church background. We started stewardship training, built around a family financial management course, soon after we opened. The church has continued a course like it year after year for more than two decades. The result has been an economic powerhouse!

The church has grown to have a capable staff and well-appointed campus, as well as support multiple mission trips annually, plant multiple new churches, and give monthly and seasonal gifts to national and international mission projects. When stewardship is taught to young believers, they start growing sooner into the stewards God expects them to become. Why wait? Why delay helping them experience God's blessing that comes when money is managed wisely according to biblical principles? Stewardship is part of basic discipleship training and should be a routine, systematic, continuing component of every church's discipleship strategy. Generous churches are built that way. Generous churches are the cumulative result of generous Christians who have learned how to manage God's money wisely.

Practice Proportional Giving

The tithe, 10 percent of gross income, is the foundation of personal giving for Christians today. Some argue tithing was an Old Testament concept, part of the law fulfilled by Jesus, therefore no longer applicable. That's a puzzling conclusion. When Jesus fulfilled the law, He filled it full in every way—meaning He exceeded its requirements and demands. The same is true for tithing. Christian giving *is* grace giving, meaning more than the tithe and exceeding the requirements of the law. Christians have the privilege of giving according to their ability, exceeding the tithe, while preserving the principle of proportional giving from the resources God entrusts to them. When people claim the tithe is no longer applicable, in a sense they are right. But only if they also believe the new standard exceeds the tithe, not as an excuse to give less.

The principle of proportional giving is the biblical pattern for individuals and families. There is no similar biblical instruction precisely for churches. Nevertheless, many churches practice proportional or percentage giving to solidify their commitment to corporate generosity. This is one way to keep a church more focused on God's kingdom than on building its own kingdom. Percentage giving ensures a church's generosity grows in proportion to its resources, while at the same time maintaining adequate funds for salaries, local programs, facility needs, and operational concerns. Every church must spend some of its resources on itself. Giving a portion of its total resources, connected to a defined percentage, helps a church maintain balance between its needs and its responsibility to help others. Percentage giving also preserves a church's mission commitments during economically challenging times. When the church has less income, it can adjust its total budget while still maintaining balanced support of both internal and external causes through proportional giving.

When we planted our church in Oregon, we contributed our first percentage-determined monthly gift through the Cooperative Program (our denomination's mission support mechanism) in July, and we didn't have our first public worship service until October. We established a pattern from the very beginning of percentage giving to missions and other outside causes. The amount was small, but this principle was implanted: we will be a generous church. The Antioch church was young when it gave money for famine relief and funded its first mission team. Giving money away to help other churches, mission programs, and kingdom projects is not the purview of large, wealthy churches. It is a step of faith for every church, including small churches with limited means. Disciplined corporate giving is an essential step toward building a generous church.

Give to Meet Human Needs

The Antioch church gave an offering to feed the hungry, meeting a basic human need. They gave to help people who, all things considered, could have been the object of their resentment rather than their love. Yet they gave generously to meet human need. Generous churches care for people in practical ways. They provide food, clothing, and shelter for people in crisis, often people who might seem unlovable.

There are multiple models for demonstrating this type of generosity. Some churches operate food pantries, clothes closets, and homeless shelters. Others cooperate with churches in their area to sponsor joint ministries. Still others contribute financially to an organization or ministry that operates independently, specializing in meeting these needs on behalf of partnering churches. When the needs are national or international (like hurricane or tsunami relief), a church may give to support missionaries or workers already in the field. In all these situations churches can also send members who participate hands on in meeting the needs of hurting people.

While care must be taken to avoid charlatans and con artists, no church should use the abuses of a few to deter compassionate action toward people in distress. Most of the world's poor suffer because of circumstances beyond their control. They deserve our help. Generous churches meet human needs. They feed the hungry, clothe the naked, and house the homeless. They visit criminals in prison, lead worship services in care facilities, and provide homes for foster children. When a natural disaster strikes, they send funds and personnel to help with recovery. Generous churches help hurting people in their community, nation, and around the world.

Give to Support Missionaries

Besides the offering for the Jerusalem church, it's also likely the Antioch church contributed financially to the missionary teams they sent out. While no specific offering is recorded for Paul and Barnabas, the church did "lay hands on them" before "they sent them off" (Acts 13:3). A commissioned blessing implying total support was extended. During the first mission trip, the team moved quickly from place to place. There is no mention of any tent-making work by the team during an extended stay in any city as later in Corinth (Acts 18:1–11). The second mission trip, this time by Paul and Silas, started in similar fashion when the team was "commended to the grace of the Lord by the brothers" (Acts 15:40). How were these teams supported? How did they pay for food, clothing, and shelter? While they sometimes worked in secular occupations (Acts 18:3), and other times enjoyed the support of new believers (Acts 16:15), it seems reasonable to assume they were at least partially supported by gifts from the brothers and sisters at Antioch.

Generous churches give money to missionaries, church planters, and others working on the edges of kingdom advance. It's tempting, once again, to defer this responsibility to large churches, denominational entities, or mission agencies. While these are part of God's plan for funding kingdom advance, all churches share this responsibility. Supporting missionaries is an important part of being a generous church.

We faced this challenge in the early years of our church in Oregon. A church planter asked if we could help fund a new church. He asked for $100 per month. Our leadership team met to discuss his request. We were surviving Sunday to Sunday, spending all the offering we received with no reserves. Our attendance was only about 125. We were trying to become a stable church ourselves, much less consider helping start another church. One of our leaders asked, "Jeff, do we even have $100 a month we could give if we wanted to?" My reply startled me! I had never thought these words, much less said them. But out spilled, "This $100 we are talking about, if we give it, we will never miss it. If we don't give it, God will see to it we never get it in the first place." Those words proved prophetic. We made the commitment and supported that church for several years. Almost immediately after our decision, God brought some people to our church with remarkable resources. Their giving vastly exceeded the paltry amount we gave away for the new church. Once again Jesus fulfilled His promise, "Give, and it will be given to you; a good measure—pressed down, shaken together, and running over—will be poured into your lap" (Luke 6:38). God delights in blessing generous churches who give to support missionaries.

Give Away People

The church at Antioch gave money but also something far more valuable. They gave away people. They sent their best leaders—Paul, Barnabas, and later others—to start churches in new locations. They sacrificed having proven pastoral leadership for the missional advance of the gospel. Generous churches today give away people, sometimes their best and brightest, to strengthen other churches, start new churches, and communicate the gospel in places it hasn't been heard. Here are some ways churches can share human resources with others.

First, send members on short-term mission assignments (lasting from a few days to a few months). These can take several forms. One is sending a team nationally or internationally to support career missionaries or local national leaders. These teams assist with specific projects requested by field personnel. Often these trips instill or awaken passion among believers for the significant needs in overseas settings resulting in long-term relationships. Workers of all ages with ministerial, professional, technical, or service skills are needed—meaning almost anyone can be useful in the appropriate setting.

Another way to deploy people on short-term assignments is to share them locally, helping a struggling church gain new strength. Many churches, for example, do events like Vacation Bible School. Sending workers already trained, with supplies in hand, to replicate this program in a neighboring congregation can make ministry possible for a smaller church incapable of hosting such a labor-intensive effort.

Churches can also share workers to temporarily strengthen another nearby church. When we launched our church in Oregon, we needed worship team members. Area churches loaned us guest singers, on a rotating basis, to buttress our worship services. They made the quality in our services far better than our small core group could have provided. Better worship experiences helped us retain people who visited our church and were surprised by the quality of the worship service in a school gym. These same churches shared child-care workers, greeters, and other support personnel in our early months. Their kindness was an invaluable contribution and encouragement to our growth.

A second way to give people away is by sending a core group of members from your church to plant a new one. One mission-minded church used an intentional strategy to start two new churches in their area. They invited the founding pastors of these two churches to join their church for one year, start a weekly Sunday night Bible study/worship service in their facility, and actively recruit individuals and families to go with the new churches when they launched. The pastor of the sponsoring church challenged members to meet the church planting pastors and seek God's will about going with them. He encouraged them, "If God calls you to go, take your time, talents, and tithes and leave. We consider you commissioned missionaries." The pastor was confident God would sustain all three churches with appropriate resources. Do you have the courage to trust God and give away your best members? Generous pastors and generous churches are open to this possibility.

Finally, a church can give away its best and brightest by encouraging members to answer God's call to missionary, pastoral, or other leadership roles. Many churches never experience the privilege and excitement of sending a person into ministry leadership. Fewer and fewer pastors seem to include "answering God's call" as one of the options during the invitation or response time in public worship. Why is this? Have we lost confidence in God's capacity to call? Do we doubt the need for people to respond to this call? God is still calling men and women of all ages into ministry leadership. A church which challenges people to consider God's call and teaches them how to understand and interpret the experience will know the joy of launching men and women into service around the world.[20]

One of my surprises as a seminary president was learning from students how many of their Christian parents oppose their answering God's call. For example, one student faced continued criticism from his father (a leader in a prominent church) for not following through on his secular career plans. He is called to international missionary service, and his parents are resolutely opposed. They want him close to home, earning a good salary, producing grandchildren, and enjoying extended family life together. Who doesn't want these things? All of us do. But God's call supersedes career plans and family relationships. God's call demands obedience. When a young person volunteers for missionary or pastoral service, the church (including Christian parents and grandparents) must rally in full support, not criticize and discourage. This includes prayer, encouragement, and financial support for college and seminary training as well as launching into ministry leadership.

Two churches, along with a few individuals in those churches, paid for my seminary training and encouraged me to prepare for a lifetime of leadership responsibility. Those friends later told me, "We knew you would leave us when you were finished with school, but we still wanted to invest in your future." Generous churches produce kingdom leaders. Generous churches teach and preach God's call. They encourage and support those who answer God's call. They know the joy of sharing in the results of God's work through those leaders as they progress through a lifetime of service.

Generous churches give away money and people to advance God's kingdom. They are disciplined givers, giving proportionately while trusting God to sustain them through good times and bad as they share resources with others. These churches are committed to developing stewards, members who understand part of being a disciple is managing finances wisely. Healthy churches measure their financial strength by how much they give away and invest in others, not by how much they amass for themselves. Transformational churches are generous churches, with members committed to sacrificing for kingdom causes.

Questions for Reflection

1. Does your church have a stewardship development program? If not, what can you do to encourage your leaders to implement one?

2. Does your church practice proportional giving? Do you think this is a healthy model for your church to adopt or strengthen? How can you help this happen?

3. Does your church give to meet human needs? Do you give personally to help with this effort? If not, why not? Does your church give to support missionaries? Do you? If not, why not?

4. Does your church send people on mission projects? Do you help neighboring churches? Does your church encourage people to answer God's call and then support them when they do? What can you do to raise the awareness about answering God's call among fellow church members?

5. On a scale of 1 to 10, how would you rate the generosity of your church? Do you consider your church to be a generous church? Why or why not? What can you do to help your church give itself away more aggressively?

Part 3

A Hopeful Conclusion

Chapter Ten

The Future of Your Church

A case-study approach to church health, while not comprehensive of all aspects of congregational life, nevertheless presents
a daunting portrait of what a church can be. No church stacks up
perfectly to the transformational model of Antioch. Most of us
can only dream of being part of a church like that. It's easy to be
discouraged, even intimidated, by comparing our churches to this
ancient model of world-impacting effectiveness. When considering
the future, it's easy to be pessimistic based on our experience with
local struggles and temporal realities. A broader perspective, not
just of the global church but also of eternal certainties, is essential
to determining an appropriate perspective on the future of local
churches.

Starting a new church and growing it to viability is one of the
most difficult leadership challenges a person can accept. Assuming
pastoral leadership of an existing church is equally difficult,
compounded by troublesome tendencies, issues, and sins existing
prior to a pastor's arrival. These inherited patterns make change
difficult and can lead to significant frustration and heartache.

Since starting and/or growing a church is so hard, why make the effort? Why give your life leading such a troubled and sometimes troublesome entity? Given the problems of the modern church, why even try to approximate the Antioch model?

While Paul helped stabilize the Antioch church, as well as start multiple others on his trips recorded in Acts, he wrote his most expansive exaltation of the church in his letter to the Ephesians. Paul helped found the church at Ephesus (Acts 19:1–20), sharing the pangs of its birth and early development. His life was threatened when his preaching about Jesus set off a full-scale riot (Acts 19:21–41). He also shared a poignant moment with the Ephesians' elders when he left them for the last time after delivering one of his longest messages preserved in the biblical record (Acts 20:17–38). The challenges these men had shared and the intimacy of their relationships set the stage for Paul's classic statement extolling the church.

Paul's praise of the church sounds poetic, more like song lyrics than words on a page. He wrote,

> This grace has been given to me—the least of all the saints!—to proclaim to the Gentiles the incalculable riches of the Messiah, and to shed light for all about the administration of the mystery hidden for ages in God who created all things. This is so that God's multi-faceted wisdom may now be made known through the church to the rulers and authorities in the heavens. This is according to the purpose of the ages, which He made in the Messiah, Jesus our Lord, in whom we have boldness, access, and confidence through faith in Him. (Eph. 3:8–12)

The crucial phrase around which this passage revolves is "through the church." Paul relates God's eternal purpose to and through the church in specific detail and in breathtaking fashion. Distilling the richness of this passage into a few paragraphs of commentary is impossible. Summarizing the main ideas, however, provides a snapshot of the biblical and theological reasons for the church's significance. In short, here are some reasons for giving your life in local church leadership.

Some might object to using this passage, which is about the church (the universal or global church), to describe the importance of the local church. But the truth communicated in this passage is more than ethereal insight into the invisible. The local church is the church expressed in tangible form and concrete terms. While these verses paint an expansive picture of the church, they also describe the churches in your community, including yours! That's often hard to believe. We know how far short the typical church seems to fall from Paul's lofty description. It's easier to accept this portrayal applying to some church somewhere else rather than the one we meet with weekly.

Your church, warts and all, may seem a far cry from the idealized description in Ephesians. Nevertheless, it's still true. The challenge for church leaders is maintaining a biblical appreciation for their church while at the same time acknowledging its shortcomings and working to overcome them. Most of this book is about the qualities of transformational churches compared and contrasted to the realities of existing churches. Let's look at a short summary of what makes your church so remarkable and worth expending life to lead.

The Church Is God's Ultimate Purpose for the Universe

Wow! That's a mouthful. The church is God's ultimate purpose for the universe. Creating humankind, redeeming believers, and sustaining them as His eternal companions is God's ultimate purpose for all He has done or will do. The church is the "administration

of the mystery hidden for ages in God who created all things"
(Eph. 3:9). God has always had a plan. His plan was a "mystery,"
not a whodunit but something so profound it's incomprehensible
apart from God. The administration or outworking of that plan
is the church. For eons God kept that concept hidden as private
knowledge contained within Himself, a true top-secret plan. His
intention was to send Jesus, the Messiah, with His "incalculable
riches" (Eph. 3:8) revealed to and enjoyed by His followers. Part of
those riches is unity with Jesus in this body and bride, the church.

The church's consummation as God's eternal companion is the
overarching purpose for the universe. The church—its creation,
preparation, and preservation—is God's purpose for everything
from Adam's creation to Armageddon's conflagration. God is
patiently shaping His eternal companion to be with Him forever.
Your church is part of God's plan, and the people in your church
will share eternity as God's companions.

The cantankerous coots, snotty-nosed kids, pimply teenagers,
and balky matrons are all part of God's eternal plan. No matter
how unlikely this seems, these people are God's eternal treasure.
He desires believers who will worship and enjoy Him forever. The
painstaking effort God made to create an entire cosmos devoted to
this one purpose boldly underscores the importance of the church.
What could be more important? Nothing even comes close to the
church, and your church, in eternal significance.

The Church Is the Full Revelation of God's Wisdom

God's wisdom exceeds human wisdom in every way. Aspects
of God's wisdom are revealed in various ways in the Bible
(described, for example, throughout the book of Proverbs). The
church, however, is the ultimate revelation of God's wisdom. Paul

declared, "God's multi-faceted wisdom may now be made known through the church to the rulers and authorities in the heavens" (Eph. 3:10). Two particularly unique aspects of God's wisdom are revealed through the church.

First, God's "multi-faceted" wisdom is revealed through the church. Imagine holding a precisely cut diamond up to a light and turning it slowly. The facets reveal different shades, shapes, and qualities of the stone. No one viewpoint contains all the stone's attributes. Each way it's viewed, new aspects are revealed. In a similar way the church unveils multiple facets of God's wisdom.

The church is more a morphing organism than a monolithic organization. It is everchanging, continually revealing new aspects of God's work among people in our world. The church is multicultural, multinational, multilingual, and multigenerational. Because of this, the church is methodologically diverse and culturally shaded. The true church has only one Lord and Leader, Jesus. Therefore, it's a volunteer movement held together by spiritual power, not a coercive collection of people dominated by hierarchical control. All of this reveals God's plan for His church, a multifaceted expression of His creativity and ingenuity culminating in a perfect companion for His infinite intricacy. The church gives us a glimpse of God's wisdom and reminds us of God's singular capacity to conceive, create, oversee, and relate to endless complexity in the universe.

Second, God's wisdom is revealed through the church "to the rulers and authorities in the heavens." Paul's cosmology includes spirit beings who inhabit nonspecific atmospheric locations "in the heavens." These rulers and authorities include both angels and demons. They are engaged in spiritual warfare impacting human affairs. In this passage, however, the focus is on their observation of the church and what it reveals to them. The church shows God's multi-faceted wisdom, in all its fullness, to these heavenly beings.

Angels and demons have an awareness of God humans don't yet share. They are part of the spiritual realm, with heavenly access and perspective. Angels and demons are created beings that exist perpetually and have observed God's activity through the ages. Paul declared that seeing the church stopped them in their tracks. Upon its revelation, a holy hush might have fallen on all of them as they collectively thought, *Well, we never saw that coming.* The mystery of the church, hidden in God for ages, astounded both angels and demons when it was revealed. Aspects of God's person and plan, not previously known or anticipated, are now fully displayed. The church is the full and final revelation of God's purpose, and even angels and demons are amazed by its existence.

Your church, even on its worst day, is still an awe-inspiring revelation to the spiritual world surrounding you. What a staggering thought! Angels and demons look at the redeemed people gathered in your worship service with holy awe, marveling at God's handiwork to create a companion people with whom He will share eternity. Particularly angels, who share close access to God, must long for the communion with the Father only His children, redeemed through Jesus, can share. Capturing this sense of wonder will help you maintain a high view of your church. It inspires heavenly awe. Certainly it should create a similar sense of wonder and appreciation in you.

The Church Is the Final Result of Jesus' Life and Work

Jesus is now among us as Savior and Lord. His saving work results in redeemed people. Those redeemed people share spiritual life, the life of Jesus, corporately expressed as the church. The final and natural outcome of Jesus' life and work is the church. Paul concluded, "[The church] is according to the purpose of the ages, which He made in the Messiah, Jesus our Lord" (Eph. 3:11).

The church is the final product, the complete outworking, of God's redemptive plan through Christ. When Jesus launched His earthly ministry, He quickly assembled twelve special disciples to begin creating the church. The focus of their training was equipping them to carry on after Jesus' resurrection. When He ascended, He instructed His followers about their responsibility to spread the gospel. The book of Acts is a history of the highlights of their obedience to Jesus. While it wasn't a smooth process, it was an effective one as early Christians formed one church after another, taking the gospel to city after city. The immediate result of Jesus' life and work was the establishment of the first churches. Their legacy has continued as the consummation and continuation of Jesus' incarnation is the perpetuity of the church.

Each of us leaves a legacy—some good, some bad. Jesus' eternal legacy from His brief earthly sojourn is all good. His legacy is the church. It could not and would not have existed unless Jesus came as the Redeemer. His unique work as the God-man made the church possible. The church, including your local church, is only possible because of Jesus' time on earth culminating in His death, burial, resurrection, and ascension. Jesus is the only One who could inaugurate the church. His uniqueness as the one and only Son of God, His willingness to exchange heaven's glory for earth's temporality, and, most of all, His unprecedented resurrection and ascension make the church possible. Jesus' legacy for the ages is the church—now His body, someday His bride.

Even from this brief biblical and theological sketch, the preeminence of the church in God's eternal order is clear. Remember, these scriptural realities don't describe some perfect church somewhere. They describe your church with all its inadequacies and idiosyncrasies. Your church is the fulfillment of God's purpose for the universe. Your church is the full revelation of God's wisdom. Your church is the final outcome and natural result of Jesus' redemptive work. Thank God for your church!

Growing out of these scriptural realities are three practical observations about the church and why its importance is unrivaled. These are additional reasons a life devoted to leading a church is a life well spent.

The Church Is Durable

The church is here to stay (until it migrates to heaven) and reigns eternally with God. The church on earth has lasted for about two thousand years. That's quite a track record for longevity. The church has endured doctrinal disasters, poor leadership, organizational mismanagement, and the waxing and waning of its missional commitment. The church has survived internal division and external assault. Spiritual warfare has consistently been waged against the church with devilish, relentless intensity. From time to time this has erupted into widespread persecution, even occasional attempts to extinguish the church altogether. On the other extreme, the church has sometimes lost its way as a spiritual organism by exchanging missional purposes for the pseudo-superior trappings of governmental partnerships. The church has faced every kind of external opposition and internal distraction possible for two millennia.

Despite all of this the church endures. It continues, in various forms and with varying levels of health, in countless nations, cities, towns, and villages around the world. The church is here to stay. While some local churches struggle and close, the Spirit is always at work assembling the redeemed at other locations. New churches are planted, and new life continually congregates in new forms. The church rolls on, overcoming the mistakes of humans and the wiles of Satan. The church is durable. Your church is part of this marching army.

The Church Is Holistic

The church, as an expression of God's wisdom, is a holistic movement. The church emerges from and belongs in "every tribe and language and people and nation" (Rev. 5:9). It's a spiritual movement eclipsing racial, geographic, linguistic, and political distinctions. The church fits in every country, culture, and subculture. The church is also multigenerational. Everyone from preschoolers to patriarchs is welcome. The church is equally accessible for men and women; no gender restrictions are placed on redemption or membership. The church is also no respecter of persons related to talents, abilities, aptitudes, status, or wealth. In fact, the church is rare among modern organizations in that it seeks out the broken, hurting, and victimized as objects of its recruitment.

The holistic nature of the church means everyone can be included. God's gift of salvation is available to all—not just the beautiful, wealthy, or influential. Church membership begins with redemption, a common experience for all believers, and isn't dependent on any accomplishment or status prior to regeneration. The church is for everyone.

Having formerly served as a pastor for many years, I am sometimes asked, "What do you miss about pastoral leadership?" One thing is working with a wide variety of people—all ages, perspectives, and problems. I miss the challenge (and occasionally, the humor) of dealing with people from all kinds of backgrounds. Another lost blessing is ministering to children, especially helping them process their understanding of salvation leading to baptism. Nothing replaces a snaggle-toothed child's scuffing her toe and saying, "Pastor, I want to be bab-a-tized," while her nervous parents look on with a strange combination of pride and anxiety. Caring for families and leading children to discover the gospel and commit themselves to Jesus is an irreplaceable blessing for pastors. Experiencing diversity in ministry opportunities to all kinds of people is one of the blessings of church leadership.

The Church Is Effective

The church is the fulfillment of Jesus' work on earth and the best venue possible for disciple making and kingdom expansion. Some might question this conclusion, given the way many churches seem to struggle to fulfill their mission. But take a global look. On some continents the church is struggling. On others it is thriving. God is moving through the global church, continually enlivening it and using it to fulfill His mission.

Churches are disciple-making organisms charged with forming the life of Jesus in believers. Local churches are spiritual-formation laboratories. We shape character, confront sin, correct poor choices, and call people to a higher plan of living. While parachurch organizations specialize in assisting a segment of believers (like college students, military personnel, or athletes), churches disciple everyone. That is simultaneously heartening and maddening for leaders who oversee this process. We know because we are people working with people, disciple-making perfection is impossible. Despite this, churches are still the most effective means for accomplishing God's mission in the world. When Christian leaders, in frustration, look for alternatives to unhealthy churches, what do they do? They plant new churches and pray for church-planting movements! There is no viable replacement for local churches as the centerpiece of God's strategic disciple-making methodology.

If you are a church detractor, a simple question is, What is your alternative strategy? It must be a comprehensive strategy for everyone, not just a select group. It must also be an eternal strategy, timeless, and timely in every era. It's easy to take shots at churches. It's much harder to create a workable alternative. Rather than waste productive time demeaning churches, our efforts are more wisely expended reforming, refining, and realigning churches. Shaping your church toward the biblical ideal will be difficult but worth the life investment required to make it happen. Local churches, even when they struggle, are still God's best laboratory for turning people into fully devoted followers of Jesus and preparing them to be God's eternal companion.

God delights in the church and local churches. He has called you to church membership and probably some form of church leadership if you have read this entire book! Thank God for your church. Dedicate yourself to helping fulfill God's unique design for its ministry. Thank God for your calling to church leadership. Courageously lead your church toward more transformational practices and patterns. Pay the price to lead change, believing God will sustain you and that your followers will benefit from moving through the pain.

God loves the church. He loves your church. He has called you to lead, for a while, His most prized possession, His eternal companion, and the object of His ultimate purpose. You are part of shaping the destiny of the universe. What could be more worthwhile as a life investment? Thank God for the church and for your church! Give your best effort to create a person-changing, community-changing, world-changing church. Give your all to create a transformational church!

Notes

1. Thom S. Rainer and Ed Stetzer, *Transformational Church* (Nashville, TN: B&H Publishing Group, 2010), 1.

2. This dating assumes Jesus' resurrection around AD 33–34 and the Antioch events described in Acts 11 and 15 occurring in mid to late 40s. For a discussion of the dating issues of these events in Acts, see Darrell Bock, *Acts: Baker Exegetical Commentary on the New Testament* (Grand Rapids, MI: Baker Academic, 2007), 29–32.

3. Scholars disagree whether this incident happened before or after the Jerusalem Council. For the purposes of this case-study approach, it really doesn't matter. The events and how they eventually concluded are the key issues for understanding transformational church functions.

4. The United Nations. "State of World Population, 2007:Unleashing the Potential of Growth," http://www.un.org/partnerships/Docs/UNFPA.

5. John Polhill, *The New American Commentary: Acts* (Nashville, TN: B&H Publishing Group, 1992), 268.

6. Ibid., 269.

7. Bock, *Acts: Baker Exegetical Commentary on the New Testament*, 413.

8. F. F. Bruce, *The New International Commentary on the New Testament: Acts* (Grand Rapids, MI: Eerdman's Publishing Co., 1981), 238.

9. Bock, *Acts: Baker Exegetical Commentary on the New Testament*, 413.

10. Polhill, *The New American Commentary: Acts*, 269.

11. Bock, *Acts: Baker Exegetical Commentary on the New Testament*, 413.

12. Brad Waggoner, *The Shape of Faith to Come* (Nashville: B&H Publishing Group, 2009), 20.

13. Ibid., 48.

14. Ibid., 276.

15. See www.lifeway.com/research, www.gallup.com, www.barna.org, or www.pewresearch.org for the latest studies on religion, church health, and spiritual practices in the United States.

16. Scholars debate the sequence and interleaving of the events in Acts 15 and Galatians 2. For our purposes, the precise order of events isn't significant. The biblical record illustrates the intensity of the conflict no matter the order of events.

17. See www.sbc.net for the full *Baptist Faith and Message 2000*.

18. Joseph Rost, *Leadership for the 21st Century* (Westport, CT: Praeger Publishers, 1991), 69.

19. For more detailed background on these three men see Polhill, *The New American Commentary: Acts,* 289–90 and Bruce, *The New International Commentary on the New Testament: Acts,* 259–61.

20. Jeff Iorg, *Is God Calling Me?* (Nashville, TN: B&H Publishing Group, 2008) explains the concept of God's call in more detail.